Soundin

Jan Bell

Longman

Longman Group UK Limited,
Longman House, Burnt Mill, Harlow,
Essex CM20 2JE, England
and Associated Companies throughout the world.

© Longman Group UK Limited 1989

First published 1989
Seventh impression 1994

Set in 9/11pt Palatino Roman
Printed in Malaysia by TCP

ISBN 0 582 79539 7

Acknowledgements

Thanks are due to:

Bruce Milne, for all the hard work he spent helping
on the book, and for all his ideas.
Kate Goldrick, for encouraging the book in the first
place, and being a most enthusiastic and
supportive editor.
Peter Marsh and Kate Lovell, for all their help and
patience.
The Bell College, Saffron Walden, for piloting some
of the material, and providing facilities for some of
the recordings.
The headmistress of Sir Thomas More primary
school, Saffron Walden, for allowing us to use their
premises and record their children.

and also to the following people for allowing us to
record them:

Ivy Baker	Cindy Leany
Stephen and Marie Bell	Pat and Helen Lodge
Sue Boardman	Stephanie Lott
David Bowker	Bruce Martin
Tony Buckby	Heather Mason
Damian Cahill	Jo Mason
Nick Charge	Robert Mercer
Helen Cox	Alistair Monk
David Eastment	Tim Moores
Karen Giblin	Roger Owens
Louisa Gold	Philip Prowse
Jenny Hogley	Sir John Ruggles-Brise
Dermot House	Simon Thompson
Mike Hughes	Brian Tomlinson
Nina Hume	Peter Watson
Helen Johnson	Barbara Webb
Ann, Melanie and Justine Lawson	

We are grateful to the following for permission to
reproduce copyright material:

The author's agents on behalf of the author, Peter
Gabriel and Cliofine Limited for the lyrics from 'Don't
Give Up' (c) 1986 Cliofine Limited; the Health
Education Authority for an extract from the leaflet
'Cycling for health' (c) Health Education Authority;
Woolworths plc for an extract from *Saffron Walden
(Herts and Essex) Observer* 11/12/86.

We are grateful to the following for permission to
reproduce copyright material:

Belgian Tourist Office/Espley & Espley Advertising
Ltd for page 47; Camera Press Ltd for page 40;
Colorific for page 42; Rob Fowler for page 14; The
Hutchison Library for page 16 (top middle);
Linguaphone/Leagas Delaney for page 23; Longman
Photographic Unit for page 34; The Photo Source for
pages 16 (top right) & 18 (left); Picturepoint-London
for pages 16 (bottom left), 16 (bottom middle), 16
(bottom right), 18 (middle) & 18 (right); Popperfoto
for page 36; Royal Society for the Prevention of
Cruelty to Animals for page 12; Sporting Pictures
(UK) Ltd for page 16 (top left); Syndication
International for page 24.

Our thanks to the following for the use of their
advertisements:

Cambridge Theatre Company; Cameron Mackintosh
Ltd; Cannon Cinemas Ltd; The Red Lion/Mid. Anglia
Newspapers Ltd; Reflections; Royal Opera House/
Design by Liz Bury & Rugantino, all for page 28.

Illustration page 32 by Chris Ryley.

The publishers would like to thank all those involved
in reporting and advising on their material in its draft
stages, and also all those UK schools involved in the
pilot study of the Longman Skills series:

London: International House; Central School; Davies
School; London School of English; Kingsway Princeton
Cambridge: Eurocentre; Anglo-World; Cambridge Academy
Edinburgh: Stevenson College; Basil Paterson; Edinburgh
Language Foundation
Eastbourne: English Centre
Torquay: Torquay International
Oxford: Godmer House; Swan School; Anglo-World
Brighton: Regent School; St. Giles' School
Bournemouth: Anglo-Continental; BEET Language Centre;
English Language Centre
Hastings: International House; EF International School
Exeter: International School

Contents

Map of the book

Unit	Text type/Topic	Listening sub-skills and language focus	Other skills developed
1 A New Job	Phone dialogue Work	**Listening:** · to check predictions · for information · intensively **Language:** · question forms · functional language · duration and indefinite past (present perfect) · intonation, stress	**Reading:** · prediction/specific information (job advert) **Speaking:** · information exchange **Writing:** · note-taking; formal letters
2 Julia's Strange Experience (1)	Story The supernatural	**Listening:** · to compare predictions · for information · intensively **Language:** · collocations/phrasal verbs · past tenses	**Speaking:** · discussion (sound sequence) **Writing:** · creative story writing
3 Snakes and Other Animals	Interview Pets (work)	**Listening:** · to check topics · intensively **Language:** · reported speech · instructions	**Reading:** · for gist/information (adverts, obituaries newspaper reports) **Speaking:** · discussion (of articles) · information exchange **Writing:** · summary; list of instructions
4 Street Life	Dialogue/informal monologue Living in a small street in Britain	**Listening:** · for gist · for information · intensively **Language:** · idiomatic/phrasal verbs · agreeing/disagreeing	**Speaking:** · discussion (from pictures) **Writing:** · description (places/people)
5 My Kind of Sport	Informal monologues Sport/leisure	**Listening:** · for gist · for information · intensively **Language:** · points of time/duration (present perfect) · comparative forms	**Speaking:** · discussion (comparing) · information exchange **Writing:** · writing a leaflet
6 Holiday Plans	Discussion Holidays/leisure	**Listening:** · for gist · for information · intensively **Language:** · future forms · idiomatic language · *Do you prefer/Would you rather*	**Reading:** · questionnaire **Speaking:** · information exchange · discussion (of pictures) **Writing:** · postcards
7 Frightening Experiences	Interview Crash (disaster)	**Listening:** · for gist · for information **Language:** · headlines in the press · passive · past tense forms	**Reading:** · matching headlines to articles **Speaking:** · discussion **Writing:** · newspaper article
8 Are You a Good Language Learner?	Lecture Language learning	**Listening:** · for main points · intensively **Language:** · modals (*have to, don't have/need to, should*)	**Reading:** · advertisement **Speaking:** · discussion (priorities) **Writing:** · designing an advert/poster
9 Children Talking	Interview Childhood/leisure	**Listening:** · for gist · for information · intensively **Language:** · modals (*have to, make/let . . . do*) · past habits (*used to*) · comparisons	**Speaking:** · information exchange **Reading:** · newspaper article **Writing:** · notes
10 Julia's Strange Experience (2)	Story The supernatural	**Listening:** · for gist · for information · intensively **Language:** · reported speech	**Speaking:** · discussion/prediction **Writing:** · story

Unit	Text type/Topic	Listening sub-skills and language focus	Other skills developed
11 A Night Out	Dialogue Telephone conversation/ leisure	**Listening:** · for gist · for information · intensively **Language:** · expressing emotion	**Reading:** · entertainments guide/diary **Speaking:** · discussion · information exchange · making plans **Writing:** · diary extract
12 A Day in the Life of . . .	Informal monologues Work	**Listening:** · for gist · for information · for interpretation · intensively **Language:** · regular habits (*will*) · comparative forms	**Speaking:** · discussion (priorities) **Writing:** · magazine article
13 A Robbery	Anecdote Crime/disaster	**Listening:** · for gist · for information **Language:** · idiomatic language · past tenses (sequencing) · describing people	**Reading:** · newspaper article **Speaking:** · discussion **Writing:** · report
14 An Interview with Sir John	Interview Royalty	**Listening:** · to check predictions · for gist · for information **Language:** · *you're not supposed to* · past conditionals	**Speaking:** · discussion (of picture) **Writing:** · menu and list
15 This Proud Land	Song Unemployment	**Listening:** · to identify words · for gist · for interpretation · intensively **Language** · sentence cohesion · phrasal verbs · sound recognition (contracted forms)	**Reading:** · interpretation (song) **Speaking:** · giving opinions/discussion **Writing:** · letter; poem/essay
16 The Supernatural	Discussion The supernatural	**Listening:** · for gist · for information **Language:** · vocabulary · giving opinions · agreeing/disagreeing	**Reading:** · questionnaire **Speaking:** · discussion **Writing:** · list and note
17 Disaster	News broadcast Disaster	**Listening:** · for gist · for information **Language:** · passive forms · past tenses	**Speaking:** · discussion (of picture) **Writing:** · dialogue/notes
18 Remembering My Schooldays	Anecdote Education	**Listening:** · to check predictions · for gist · for information · for interpretation **Language:** · past habits (*would*) · vocabulary	**Speaking:** · discussion (of picture) **Writing:** · a note
19 Radio Phone-In	Telephone dialogues Legal rights	**Listening:** · for gist · for information **Language:** · vocabulary · giving advice	**Reading:** · problem letters **Speaking:** · discussion (of letters) **Writing:** · letter
20 Places I Know	Informal monologues Places	**Listening:** · for information · intensively **Language** · conditional forms	**Speaking:** · discussion (of priorities) **Writing:** · advertisement

To the teacher

WHO IS *SOUNDINGS* INTENDED FOR?

This book is intended for intermediate students of English who want more intensive exposure to natural spoken English and who want to develop the skills necessary for listening with confidence to this unsimplified language.

It also provides students with an opportunity to develop their speaking, writing and reading skills and to extend their range of vocabulary, revise their knowledge of grammar and learn something about British life.

Although this book is particularly useful for class-study it can also be used by self-study students.

THE RECORDINGS

The book consists of twenty units, each intended to take around fifty minutes. Each unit has a different topic, although many of these are linked thematically, and the topics have been chosen to stimulate maximum interest. There is a wide variety of text types; almost all of them are unscripted and recorded out of the studio so that the language is natural and spontaneous, with all the features of natural connected speech as well as a range of accents, different speeds of talking and different levels of formality. Most recordings last for around three minutes.

GENERAL PRINCIPLES BEHIND THE BOOK

All of the units are divided into three main parts.

A Before listening   The activities in this section aim to:
● introduce learners to the topic and arouse motivation
● encourage prediction skills based on knowledge of the world and the topic
● activate or introduce areas of vocabulary
● develop speaking skills
● develop reading skills

B While listening   The activities in this unit aim to:
● develop confidence in listening to unsimplified language by giving students a genuine communicative purpose for listening (in the form of a listening activity)
● encourage students to develop strategies relevant to their purpose for listening, for example, some tasks will focus on understanding the general sense, listening for specific information, or interpreting attitude rather than trying to understand every word
● focus on going from global to more detailed understanding (this will require the tape to be played at least twice)
● train students to deduce the meaning of new words in context
● focus on *the process* of how students got the answer rather than on what answer they got (teaching rather than testing)

C Writing task   These activities aim to:
● provide the learners with a communicative purpose and stimulus for writing different text types, focusing on creativity as well as accuracy
● give the students an opportunity to focus on specific linguistic forms or areas of vocabulary which have been brought up in the unit

LANGUAGE FOCUS

Most units highlight some aspect of language as it is used in the text, whether it is an area of grammar, vocabulary, functional meaning or phonology. Listening to the tape again after the lesson, with the aid of the transcript if necessary, can help students develop a 'feel' for English stress and intonation patterns and to become more aware of language in use.

ALSO INCLUDED IN THE BOOK

- transcripts of the recordings
- a key to the activities
- teachers notes – more detailed notes on units where considered necessary
- a 'Map of the book'

CONCLUSION

This book would be a useful supplement to any coursebook on a regular course where skills development is seen as an important and regular component of a teaching programme.

On a shorter course it could be used on its own, to activate language already studied and systematically develop language skills in general, and listening in particular.

To the student

All of the recordings in this book are of 'real people'. They range from young children to old people and talk about different topics such as ghosts and pets. The texts are not simplified; all the people talk at natural speed, in a variety of different accents and often using informal idiomatic language.

Listening is a difficult but very important communication skill. The tasks which accompany the recordings give you a purpose for listening. They help to train you to listen for a particular reason and not to panic if you do not understand every word. The aim is to build up your skills systematically and to develop the confidence to listen selectively and efficiently.

Included in every unit are writing and speaking activities and often there are reading activities too. In each unit there is plenty of opportunity for vocabulary extension and revision of different aspects of language.

This book is best used in class where you can interact with other students. However, it can also be used by students studying alone – there is a key to the exercises so that you can check your answers.

We hope you find the book useful and interesting.

A New Job

Sue has decided that she would like to change her job and sees this advert in her local newspaper.

HOST/HOSTESS

Walk into Woolworths and you will feel the difference. An atmosphere of change is sweeping the Company, bringing better stores, new high quality merchandise, and higher levels of customer service. Perhaps even more important, our new style is making working for Woolworths fun.

To help achieve this we need a friendly, obliging person to take care of our busy, hardworking staff and maintain excellent catering standards in your local store.

Running our small staff dining room, you will be preparing and serving simple hot and cold meals, in a modern, well-kept kitchen, at break and lunch times. Some catering experience is necessary but a happy, outgoing manner is equally important.

In return for your contribution we offer a competitive salary plus benefits and the chance to work in a friendly, family environment.

Why wait? Work with Woolworths now!

Applications in writing or by phone to:
The Personnel Officer,
F. W. Woolworth plc.,
17–21 Potter Street,
Bishop's Stortford,
Herts CM23 3UN.
Tel: Bishop's Stortford 51108.

WOOLWORTHS
The shop which has something for everyone

PART *A*

Before you listen

1) Look at the headline for the job advertised above. What kind of job do you think a 'host/hostess' is?

2) Now read the text to find out the following:
a) What kind of company is 'Woolworths'? Which words tell you this?
b) What does the job involve doing?
c) What should you do next if you are interested in the job?

3) Imagine you are Sue and you are making notes of other things you want to know about the job. Write your questions here.

a) _____
b) _____
c) _____

PART *B*

Listening activities

4) Listen to Sue's phone conversation and see if the questions which you wanted to know were answered.

5) Listen again.
a) Work in pairs (A and B). One of you should fill in the notes which Sue wanted to find out, the other should fill in John Adams's memo form.

Sue's notes

A
To find out:
- Salary?
- Hours?
- Duties?
- Number of staff
- Interview? When?

John Adams's form

```
                                      MEMO
    JOB APPLICATIONS
 B                                    Name
    Surname (Mr/Miss/Mrs)
                                      Present employer:
    Catering experience              Name
                                      Job

    Possible for interview?          Interview date/time
    Comments (if any)
```

b) Exchange the information you have written down with your partner.

6) Read and complete these mini-dialogues using what you remember from the text.

a) **Operator:** Hello, Woolworths!

      Sue: Ah hello. I wonder _____

            the Personnel Manager, please?

 Operator: Yes, certainly. If _____ a minute

            I'll put you through.

      Sue: Thank you.

b) **John Adams:** _____ experience in catering?

      Sue: Yes . . . I'm at present working for and _____

            _____ the same firm for about five years, for a small firm

            of consultant engineers and _____ work rather

            similar to the kind . . . described in the advertisement.

c) **John Adams:** Perhaps _____ for an interview some

            time?

      Sue: Yes, when _____ for you?

 John Adams: _____ next Wednesday?

      Sue: Yes, I think _____ fine, actually.

7) Now listen again and compare your answers in 6) to what is said on the tape.

PART C

Writing task

Imagine that Sue decided to *write* to John Adams rather than telephoning. Using the information in the text, and adding any extra information you like, write a short formal letter. Use the format below:

```
Personnel manager,               Sue's address
Name and address of company,              Date


Dear Sir or Madam,




Yours faithfully,
```

Include the following points in your letter:
- why you are writing/how you heard about the job
- information about your experience in catering
- other relevant information (hobbies, travel abroad, qualifications, etc.)
- information you would like to know

Before you listen

1) Your teacher will play a few sounds to you. As you listen, make a note of what these sounds are. Make the notes in English or your own language, and ask your teacher to explain any new vocabulary you need. Then discuss with your partner what you think the story is going to be about.

Listening activities

2) Listen to the story once. Were your predictions correct?

3) Listen again and decide whether the following statements are true (T) or false (F) according to the text. Write your answer in the appropriate box.

a) Julia was going to a party. ☐

b) She was alone in her car. ☐

c) She stopped her car because she was lost. ☐

d) Julia saw the cat because there was a full moon. ☐

e) The cat ran away as soon as Julia got out of the car. ☐

f) Julia was wet and cold. ☐

g) She decided to spend the night in the car because she was lost. ☐

h) To pass the time until morning she listened to the radio. ☐

i) She stopped feeling nervous. ☐

j) The rain woke her up. ☐

4) Match the adjectives from Column A to the nouns in Column B to make phrases which come from the text. The first one is done for you.

COLUMN **A**		COLUMN **B**
i) wild, stormy	e	a) rain
ii) lonely	☐	b) engine
iii) clear	☐	c) encounter
iv) strange	☐	d) object
v) large, black	☐	e) night
vi) dead	☐	f) idea
vii) pouring	☐	g) country lane

5) Try to make ten sentences from the text by using one of the words from Column A, one of the verbs from Column B and *possibly* (but not always) a word from Column C. (*Note:* If you add one from Column C you will sometimes need a preposition.)

Example: The waves crashed against the cliffs.

COLUMN **A**	COLUMN **B**		COLUMN **C**
The waves	was opening	in	the torch
The rain	turned up	against	the cliffs
The trees	swayed		the sea
The lightning	crashed		the music
Julia (×5)	stretched		the wind
The cat	lit up		the engine
Someone	picked up		the windscreen
	shivered		the passenger door
	switched off		
	beat		
	screamed		

a) The rain _____

b) The trees _____

c) The lightning _____

d) Julia _____

e) Julia _____

f) Julia _____

g) Julia _____

h) Julia _Switch off_ _____

i) The cat _____

j) Someone _____

6) Listen to the story again and check your answers to questions 4) and 5).

PART C

Writing task

Write the rest of the story. You can do it on your own or with a partner. Begin like this:

Julia screamed _____

Snakes and Other Animals

A

What's it worth to save a cat?

When our Inspector found Fluff she was close to death. The victim of deliberate cruelty and neglect, she had been roaming wild for months.

The Inspector didn't waste a second. He knew saving Fluff's life wouldn't be easy. But for him, the animal was all that mattered.

He didn't stop to count the cost. It took many months of careful feeding and attention before Fluff was restored to health. But finally the time came when she could be placed in the kind of loving home she deserved.

You wouldn't expect anything else from the RSPCA. Preventing cruelty and rescuing animals in distress is what we're all about.

And if we didn't do it, who would? Our work is entirely dependent on people like you. A gift from you today would help us to provide more

Inspectors and prevent animal cruelty. And that would mean we could do even more to save lives.

RSPCA

Return coupon with your donation to RSPCA, FREEPOST, Causeway, Horsham, West Sussex RH12 1ZA.

I support the work the RSPCA does to save animals in distress. Please use my donation wherever it is most needed. I enclose:

£100 ☐   £50 ☐   £25 ☐   £15 ☐   £10 ☐   Other £ _____

I wish to donate via Visa/Access Card _____

Signature _____ Date _____

Name _____

Address _____

Postcode _____

Charity in Action

B

In Memory

Kipper – In loving memory of our beautiful and adored Siamese, missing now for over a year. We miss you and love you more than you will ever know, and never give up hope that you will return.
          Love from Mum and Dad

Catty (Gobolino) – my beloved baby, put to sleep after a long illness, at the age of 13½. The house seems so empty without you, my darling.
     Until we meet again, your Lucy.

Basil – a much loved puss, cruelly taken from me on November 3rd, 1986. You brought so much light and happiness into my life – will I ever stop mourning you? Rest in peace safely with little Percy.
                    Barbara

Monty – Four years later we still see your beautiful green eyes everywhere. To our very dear and special friend who will never be forgotten by her feline and her human friends.
          Mummy, Daddy, Fluff, Henry and Mouse

PART A

Before you listen

1) Extract A:
a) Look at the pictures on the left in this advertisement. Why do you think the cat looks like this?
b) What do you think the purpose of this newspaper text is? Read it quickly once and see if you are correct.
c) What is the RSPCA?
d) Would you ever contribute to a charity like this? Why?/Why not?
e) Do you have similar organisations in your own country? What are they?

2) Extract B:
a) What do you think these extracts are and where do they come from?
b) What is your reaction to people who write things like this? Do you think they are stupid/mad, or do you think it is normal?
c) What kind of pets do you/people in your country keep?
d) What do you think the British attitude to pets is, compared to your own country?

PART B

Listening activities

3) Listen to Mr Mercer, a local vet, being interviewed. At the top of the next page is a list of things the interviewer wanted to discuss, but unfortunately we didn't have time for everything. Put a tick (✔) next to the topics which you would like to hear about in Column A.

	COLUMN A	COLUMN B
• the problems he has with pets' owners	☐	☐
• how people treat pets	☐	☐
• how much it costs to keep a dog	☐	☐
• the good things about being a vet	☐	☐
• snakes	☐	☐
• the dangers of his job	☐	☐
• how pets can be good for you	☐	☐
• how to feed a cat	☐	☐
• the sort of animals he looks after	☐	☐

Now listen, and tick the topics which *were* discussed in Column B.

4) Read the following article that a journalist wrote after having interviewed Mr Mercer about his job. Then listen to the interview again and underline or make a note of any parts where you think the journalist has not reported the interview accurately. (There are nine differences.)

JOB WATCH: ANIMALS AND THEIR OWNERS

■ Mr Robert Mercer speaks about his job as a veterinary surgeon.

Mr Mercer is a very experienced veterinary surgeon. He is qualified to deal with many different kinds of animals – either in his surgery or in various places like zoos and the jungle. He is particularly fond of snakes and keeps one as a pet. He admires them because they are strong and muscular and he finds them useful for frightening other people with! They once had to deal with a snake that was fifteen feet long; Mr Mercer was worried in case it bit him!

He feels that far too many people treat their pets too well. Some of them even kiss them! However, he believes that animals are particularly useful as companions for old people; they perform the function of friends and they can be with them the whole time. He particularly recommends budgerigars as pets for old people. When animals come to his surgery they are often frightened and can become aggressive. He is always being hurt – sometimes badly – by dogs and cats.

Mr Mercer enjoys his job and the variety it gives him. He enjoys working in his surgery, working in his office and going out on visits. His greatest love, however, is helping animals to give birth.

5) Write a summary of the interview, reporting Mr Mercer's words correctly this time. Begin like this:

In his interview with us, Mr Mercer said . . .

PART C

Writing task

You are going away for a week and your friend has very kindly offered to come in and look after your pet for you while you are away. Leave a list of instructions for your friend (Oliver) telling him what and when to feed your pet (a dog, cat, snake, or whatever pet you want) and any special needs it has. Include the following language in your instructions:
• Remember to . . .
• Don't forget . . .
• Make sure . . .

Street Life

Before you listen

This is a photograph of Mill Lane – a little street in a small market town in Britain. Look at the picture and see how many of the following questions you can answer.

1) What is another name for small houses like this (usually old)?

2) What do you call houses which are all joined together like this?

3) What do you think are the advantages and disadvantages of living in a place like this?

4) What kind of people would you expect to live there?

Listening activities

5) During our discussion with Peter and Helen, two of the people who live in Mill Lane, we talked about:
a) the advantages of living in a place like this
b) the kind of people who live there
c) the problems of pets in the lane
d) whether there was any gossip in the lane
e) the problem of noise
Listen to all the extracts once and match the number of the extract with the topic of discussion (a, b, c, d or e).

Extract one ☐   Extract two ☐   Extract three ☐

Extract four ☐   Extract five ☐

6) Listen again and complete the following exercise.

a) What is the problem with Peter's neighbours?

   i) they're old ☐

   ii) they argue a lot ☐

   iii) they shout loudly, and the walls are thin ☐

b) What is the problem with his other neighbour?

    i) he comes home at two o'clock in the morning ☐

    ii) he has a bird as a pet ☐

    iii) he plays music until late at night ☐

c) What are the problems with pets in the lane?

    i) Helen's dog makes messes in the gardens ☐

    ii) the cats fight and wake Peter up ☐

    iii) the dogs chase the cats ☐

d) The people who live in Mill Lane:

    i) have the same kind of jobs ☐

    ii) are generally the same age ☐

    iii) work unusual hours ☐

e) The advantage of living here is:

    i) it's near the shops ☐

    ii) it's quite safe from thieves ☐

    iii) everyone notices what everyone else is doing ☐

f) The police were called:

    i) because a neighbour's daughter was drunk ☐

    ii) because blue lights were flashing ☐

    iii) because a neighbour's ex-husband wouldn't go away ☐

7) Listen to extract three again and notice how Peter disagrees and later agrees with Helen. Write down his exact words.

Disagrees ⎯⎯⎯⎯⎯⎯⎯⎯⎯⎯⎯⎯⎯⎯⎯⎯⎯⎯

Agrees ⎯⎯⎯⎯⎯⎯⎯⎯⎯⎯⎯⎯⎯⎯⎯⎯⎯⎯⎯

8) The following are some of the idiomatic expressions used in the text.

Who was   ● blind drunk

              ● stone deaf

              ● shrieking at the top of her voice

Who were ● on at each other?

Who is   ● a nightbird

              ● well-looked-after?

Who   ● would *go berserk* if the dog *made messes* in their gardens?

9) Can you explain the expressions in question 8 in your own words (in English, or in your own language)? You may need to listen to the text again.

PART C

Writing task

Write a description of the area where you live (or used to live), and include a description of any interesting or unusual neighbours, gossip or events.

My Kind of Sport

A
B
C

D
E
F

Before you listen

1) Name all the sports in the photographs using the verb (e.g. to *play* tennis).

2) Which of these do you do or would you like to do/play?

3) Which of these sports do you find the most/least enjoyable, and why?

4) Which of the sports above do you think requires
a) the most skill?
b) the most stamina?

Listening activities

5) You will hear three people talking about their favourite sport. Match each of the extracts to the relevant photograph above (A, B, C, D, E or F).

Extract one: (Jo)   ☐

Extract two: (Brian)   ☐

Extract three: (Stephanie)   ☐

6) Read the following expressions. Before listening, see if you can remember or guess which description matches which sport. Then listen again to see if you were correct. The first one is done for you.

According to the texts, which sport:

- needs a lot of energy   ___squash___
- is exciting   ___foo___
- can be dangerous   ___ski___
- is very popular at the moment   ___sq___
- is fast   ___ski___
- requires skill   ___ft / ski___
- can you not play for a long time because it's tiring   ___sq___
- is expensive   ___ski___

7)

	JO	BRIAN	STEPHANIE
a) When did these people begin playing their sport?	Qulte yng	Nrly 40yr	Sino can vant bw
b) Do they still play now (yes or no)?	Yer	Yer	Yer

c) Write down exactly what they say about the length of time they have played their sport. You will need to listen to this part again.

Jo: _____

_____

Brian: _____

_____

Stephanie: _____

_____

PART C

Writing task

Read the extract below. It is from a leaflet which is trying to persuade people of the advantages of cycling for their health. Now think of one sport which *you* think is good for your health. Write a similar extract to be included in a doctor's leaflet which aims to make people healthier. Use the 'Cycling' text as a model for your extract.

FOR HEALTH

AEROBICS ON A SADDLE

Having stamina, the ability to keep the body going, means having efficient muscles, good circulation and a strong heart. Exercises
5 which are good for building stamina involve moving your arms or legs rhythmically. This creates a demand for oxygen, so the heart works a little harder, and the lungs
10 are fully used. They pump oxygen into the bloodstream, so that it passes through the heart and reaches the working muscles. Sometimes this is called aerobic
15 exercise, and cycling is an excellent form of aerobics.

THE WEIGHT OFF YOUR FEET

Stamina-building is not the only advantage of cycling. Because you're not carrying the weight of
20 your body on your feet, it's a good form of exercise for people with painful feet, bad backs, or arthritis.

And, of course, cycling can save
25 money and provide pleasure. More and more people are taking to their bikes as an alternative to driving or using public transport. Whether you're shopping, going
30 to work or travelling for pleasure, it's a lot cheaper and much

healthier! You don't have to pay for parking or petrol and it's much quicker than walking.

35 Cycling is something that all the family can enjoy.

Holiday Plans

What is your ideal holiday?

1 Do you prefer going to:
   a) the seaside
   b) a big city
   c) the countryside/mountains
   d) a place of historical or cultural importance?

2 Would you rather spend the day:
   a) sunbathing and swimming
   b) travelling around, sightseeing
   c) walking, climbing, etc.
   d) visiting museums, art galleries, etc?

3 Would you rather travel:
   a) by plane
   b) by car
   c) by train
   d) by ship/boat?

4 Do you prefer to go on holiday:
   a) alone
   b) with one friend/girlfriend/boyfriend
   c) with your family
   d) with a group of friends?

5 In the evening would you rather:
   a) go to discos/nightclubs
   b) visit local restaurants
   c) go to theatres, cinemas
   d) go to bed early?

6 Do you prefer to stay:
   a) in a luxury hotel
   b) in a self-catering apartment
   c) in a small hotel/bed & breakfast place
   d) on a camping site?

PART **A**

Before you listen

1) Do this quiz yourself. Tick the appropriate answers.

2) Do it with a partner and see whether you would make good travelling companions.

3) Look at the pictures below and choose the place that you think would be most suitable for you and your partner, if you were going on holiday together. Give your reasons.

A

B

C

PART **B**

Listening activities

4) Listen to the discussion once, and decide which of the three types of holiday in the photographs above each of these people want, and why.

Alistair: _____

Barbara: _____

Mike: _____

5) Listen again and make notes on where the three people are going to go, and what they are going to do there.

	WHERE?	HOW THEY'LL SPEND THEIR TIME
a) Alistair		
b) Barbara		
c) Mike		

6) Can you remember *exactly* how the three people talked about their future plans and which verb form they used? Try to complete the a) sentences below.

Alistair: a) _____ at eight tomorrow morning.

b) _____

Barbara: a) _____ to Tenerife _____ to Greece.

b) _____

Mike: a) _____ in the car.

b) _____

Now listen, and write down exactly what they say in the b) blanks above. Why do they use different ways of expressing the future?

7) The following sentences are taken from the text. Can you replace the word or phrase *in italics* with one of your own? You may need to listen to the tape again, to help you.

a) Well, *I'm off* tomorrow – (going to) Italy.

b) (I) might go to Greece, I haven't really *made up my mind*.

c) . . . you're not a *culture vulture* like myself?

d) . . . *dropping into* a bar at lunchtime, on the beach . . .

e) . . . *self-catering* – don't trust anyone else's food . . .

f) . . . if it's really *chucking it down* I'll go out in the car . . .

PART C

Writing task

This is the postcard that Mike sent Barbara from the Lake District. Read it, and then, using it as a model, write the one that you think *either* Barbara *or* Alistair sent to Mike.

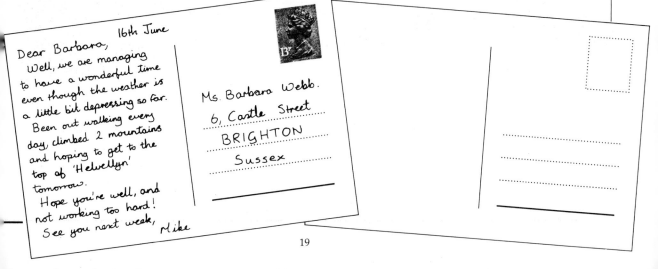

> 16th June
>
> Dear Barbara,
> Well, we are managing to have a wonderful time even though the weather is a little bit depressing so far. Been out walking every day, climbed 2 mountains and hoping to get to the top of 'Helvellyn' tomorrow.
> Hope you're well, and not working too hard!
> See you next week,
> Mike
>
> Ms. Barbara Webb.
> 6, Castle Street
> BRIGHTON
> Sussex

Frightening Experiences

A Earthquake in Ecuador

D Etna erupts again!

B Motorists trapped in floods

C Tidal wave fear, as earthquake shakes Japan

E Hurricane Harry hits Texas

F 5 dead and 20 injured in motorway horror

1 ☑

The torrential rain which has been falling now for the last four days has resulted in many people in the south-east of Britain being unable to leave their homes. Many roads are flooded, with cars and other vehicles unable to move.

2 ☐

In the town of Alice, Texas, terrified residents have shut themselves in their homes in preparation for the arrival of the 100 mph wind known as 'Hurricane Harry' which could bring disaster to the area.

3 ☐

Rosina Capputto was in tears yesterday as she watched the home she and her husband had worked so hard to build on the slopes of the volcano they love so much being engulfed by boiling lava. 'They promised me it was safe,' she sobbed.

4 ☐

Thousands of people are homeless in the South American country of Ecuador today after Friday night's tragic earthquake – the third in two years – which killed more than a thousand people and caused thousands of buildings to collapse.

5 ☐

Careless driving in foggy weather was the cause of last night's horrific accident on the M4, say police. Warnings had been given, but motorists chose to ignore them. Five people, including one child, are in a serious condition in hospital.

6 ☐

Thursday's dreadful earthquake in Japan has brought panic to the west coast of the United States as California prepares for the tidal wave which is expected to break on or near the coast around Saturday.

PART **A**

Before you listen

1) Match the headlines above to the text they relate to.

2) Discuss with your partner any frightening experiences or natural disasters which you or a friend have been involved in.

3) Look at the headlines again, and make them into complete sentences. Which verb form do you use, and why?

Listening activities

4) Listen to Brian talking about a frightening experience he was involved in in Africa. What kind of experience was it?

5) Listen again and decide whether the following statements are true (T) or false (F).

a) The accident happened in the middle of the country. ☐

b) The bus was nearly empty. ☐

c) It happened shortly after leaving the bar. ☐

d) The bus crashed into something else. ☐

e) Brian was hurt. ☐

f) People began to shout and panic. ☐

g) The driver was killed. ☐

h) Everyone got off the bus. ☐

i) No one was hurt. ☐

j) They went to hospital immediately. ☐

6) The following sentences come from the text. Try to guess what the words *in italics* mean in the context (try to find another word in English, or use your own language).
a) When we eventually *set off* from that place the driver got up speed.
b) I remember *grabbing hold* of a handle.
c) There was a *dead silence*.
d) Everyone *crawled out* through the back window.
e) People began to collapse and become *unconscious*.

PART **C**

Writing task

Imagine you are a newspaper reporter who has just interviewed Brian about his experience in the bus crash. Write a short article for your local newspaper (and don't forget to invent a headline). You can use the newspaper articles above to give you ideas.

Are You a Good Language Learner?

Before you listen

1) What do you think are the qualities of a good language learner? Put a number next to the qualities which *you* think are relevant (1 = most relevant) and add any others you can think of.

- intelligence ☐
- a certain kind of personality (what kind?) ☐
- motivation/enthusiasm ☑ *1*
- a good memory ☑ *2*
- ability to work hard ☑ *3*
- other (what?)_____ ☐
  _____ ☐
  _____ ☐

2) Discuss your choices in pairs and see if you can agree on the four most important qualities. Discuss what you
a) have to be/have
b) don't need to be/have
c) should be/have

Listening activities

3) You are going to listen to a lecture on 'The Good Language Learner', given by the Principal of a language school to a group of foreign students who have come to study English in England.
Listen, and make a note of the four main points he refers to.

Point one: _Motivation   enthusiasm_
Point two: _Personality_
Point three: _learning skill_
Point four: _Independence_

4) Which does *he* regard as the most important? Do you agree?

Motivation   yes

5) Listen to the text again, and complete the following notes that a student made.

The Good Language Learner

Classroom learning could be much more effective if we thought more about how people learn languages successfully [1]_____ .

What is a good language learner?

1 <u>Different types of motivation</u>

Instrumental (or [2] <u>external</u>) motivation   *opposite*   Integrative motivation

for example [3] <u>school, examination</u>   *is*   for example [4] <u>immigration course</u>

Integrative motivation is probably best for [5]_____ of learning.

2 <u>Personality</u>

Not necessary to be [6] <u>extravert</u> but important to be [7] <u>confidence</u>

3 <u>Learning skills</u>

Abilities include: a) [8] <u>having a good memory</u>
    b) revising efficiently
    c) monitoring your [9]_____
    d) [10]_____

4 <u>Independence</u>

([11]_____ factor, according to him)

Very important to be independent of the [12]_____ and accept [13]_____ for learning, otherwise you make no [14] <u>progress</u>

PART **C**

Writing task

Look at the advertisement below for a language study course. Imagine that you are designing a similar advert or poster to advertise *your* language school which you have just opened. Sell it as well as you can, including all the facilities you have for learning languages well and which you think are important for successful language learning.

Children Talking

1937

- No shoes, hand-me-down clothes
- Walked miles to school
- Wind-up gramophones for George Formby hits
- Cold house, poor lights, no television
- Cash from taking back empty bottles
- Holidays were trips fruit-picking
- Bread and jam for tea
- In bed by 7.30

1987

- Smart, fashionable clothes
- Lifts to school in dad's car
- Personal stereos to listen to Madonna
- TV computer games in own room
- About £3.50 pocket money per week
- Most have been abroad at least once
- Fast food TV dinners
- In bed by 10.30

PART *A*

Before you listen

Look at the picture of the two ten-year-old children in 1937 and 1987. They show what conditions were like for the average child 50 years ago compared to today.

1) Think of questions to ask your partner about his/her life when he/she was ten.
Examples: What time did you have to go to bed?
Did you use to wear nice clothes?
What would you spend your pocket money on?

2) Ask your partner the questions and make a comparison, e.g. Who had stricter parents? Who got more pocket money? etc.

3) Is the (1987) list in the picture above typical of a ten-year-old in your country? In what ways are they the same? In what ways are they different?

Listening activities

4) You are going to listen to Bruce talking to two ten-year-old children, Simon and Louisa. Below are some of the topics they discuss. Number the order in which they are talked about.

- free time ☐
- music ☐
- pocket money ☐
- going abroad ☐
- food ☐
- bedtime ☐
- rules ☐

5) Listen again and fill in the following chart with information from the text.

	SIMON	LOUISA
How much pocket money do they get?		
What do they spend it on?		
How do they spend their spare time?		
What time do they go to bed?		
Are there any other rules at home?		
Have they been abroad? If so, where?		

6) Listen again to Simon talking about his parents' rules for bedtime and other things. What does he say about:

- going to bed { during the week _____
  { at the weekend _____
- eating the food he doesn't like _____
- playing football in the back garden _____
- leaving his toys around _____

7) Think about when you were a child. Write down a few examples of things:

- you had to do _____
- were not allowed to do _____
- your parents made you do _____

Writing task

You have become famous and the radio and television want to interview you about your childhood. Select the most important events and write a press release to be given to the newspaper. Write it in the form of notes. Include:

- what you used to do
- what you did sometimes
- what your parents made you do/let you do
- what you had to do/were not allowed to do
- how you felt about members of your family

Julia's Strange Experience (2)

Before you listen

Your teacher will play the first few lines of the next part of the story. In pairs or groups, predict what you think will happen next, and tell the rest of the class.

PART **B**

Listening activities

A

B

C

D

E

F

G

H

1) Listen to the story and put the pictures in the order in which they happened. The first one has been done for you.

1 [F]   2 [D]   3 [H]   4 [A]   5 [E]   6 [G]   7 [C]   8 [B]

2) The following text is a summary of the story, as Julia's friend told it to somebody else. Unfortunately she got it wrong. Can you spot the *ten* differences between *her* version and what *really* happened?

> The person who opened the door was a woman of about twenty, wearing a raincoat and a bright blue scarf around her head to protect her from the rain. She looked quite friendly, so Julia asked her if she knew of a house where she could phone from and the woman offered to show her.
>
> They walked off together, not saying very much, and then they saw a large house with the lights still on, even though it was well after midnight. The woman rang the bell and then explained the situation to the old man who answered the door.

The ten differences:

1 _fourty_   6 _ahead_____
2 _blazer raincoat_   7 _____
3 _bright spotted scarf_   8 _knocked the door_
4 _really_   9 _dark_
5 _phone box_   10 _appeared_

3) Look at the text again and write down the *exact words* used when:

a) Julia explained that her car wouldn't start.

_____

b) She asked whether there was a phone box near there.

_____

c) The woman offered to take her there.

_____

d) Julia apologised for waking the old man up.

_____

e) He invited Julia to go in.

_____

f) He denied having children.

_____

4) What rules do we follow when we are reporting speech? Can you form any conclusions? Now rewrite the sentences in question 3) using 'said' or 'asked'. *Example:* Julia said, 'My car won't start.'

PART C

Writing task

Write a 'strange experience' story of your own, using the following words:

rats	wind	'Don't look behind'	sweat
the last bus	a broken glass	a woman in red	

A Night Out

NIGHTCLUBS

REFLECTIONS
New Cocktail Bar.
Cocktails, Spirits & Beers.
Offering the latest in
sound and lighting systems.
at the KINGS ARMS,
425 NEW KINGS ROAD,
FULHAM, SW6
736 2324

PUBS

The Red Lion Hixton
16th Century Public house
Delicious Traditional Home Cooking in
our cosy, candlelit Restaurant.
with
Extensive Menu
including exciting new fish dishes
(fresh fish from Lowestoft)
Your Old Favourites
Steaks cut to order
ALSO
BAR SNACKS · REAL ALE
FINE WINES
Please head to ensure seats
Large garden. Extension to car park
TEL: SAFFRON WALDEN
30601

RESTAURANTS

M&Fish
FRESH FISH RESTAURANT
FULLY LICENSED
We only serve Fresh Fish – Not Frozen
393 Upper Richmond Rd. Putney. SW5
(Near Dover House Rd). Tel: 876 3083
Daily deliveries from Hillingsgate
See Seafood Listings for Details

Cosy, Candle-lit
Italian Restaurant
Excellent a la Carte Menu
3 Course Meal £6.95
Speciality:
Home-made Pasta £2.65
Opening Hours
12–3pm   6–12am
Also available for
Private Parties (Max 30)
26 ROMILLY STREET, W1
TEL. 437 5302/734 9854

CINEMAS

CANON CINEMAS
CAMBRIDGE 64537
① Paul Newman, Tom Cruise
THE COLOUR OF MONEY [15]
Sep perfs wk 2.15, 5.00, 8.00
Sun 5.00, 8.00
Late show Sat 28th
Doors open 10.45 pm

② Oliver Reed,
Amanda Donohoe
THE CASTAWAY [15]
Sep perfs wk 2.00, 4.45, 7.45
Sun 4.45, 7.45

VICTORIA CAMBRIDGE 352677
① Paul Hogan
CROCODILE DUNDEE [15]
Sep perfs wk 2.00, 5.00, 8.00
Sun 5.00, 8.00

② **THE FLY [18]**
Sep perfs wk 2.15, 5.15, 8.15
Late show Friday Matt Dillon
REBEL [15]
10.45
Special one day only 26th April
2pm to 10.30 STAR TREK 1, 2, 3, 4
Adults 16, child £3 Book now!
ALL PROGS SUBJECT TO LATE CHANGE

CONCERTS

MICHAEL JACKSON
AT WEMBLEY STADIUM
Live
JULY 25TH 1988

Nigel Kennedy
with
THE WREN CHAMBER ORCHESTRA
of London

OPERA

The Royal Opera
The Los Angeles Music Center Opera production of
SALOME
RICHARD STRAUSS
New Production
Conductor Christoph von Dohnányi
Producer Peter Hall
Design & Lighting John Bury
Choreography Elizabeth Keen
Cast includes
Maria Ewing
Robert Hale Robert Tear
Helga Dernesch Robin Leggate
Tomorrow & April
14, 18, 26*, 30*
at 8.00pm
*Royal Opera House
Midland Bank Promo Performance
at least 350 £4.00 prom places
available on the night!
All performances have English surtitles
Royal Opera House
01-240 1066/1911
65 Rear Amphitheatre seats at
10.80 available on the day ex April
26 & 30 to personal callers at
Box Office from 10.00am
1 per applicant.

MUSICALS

Les Misérables
THE MUSICAL SENSATION
PALACE THEATRE
OPEN ALL HOURS
01-379 4444
24 HR CREDIT CARD-BKG FEE
FIRST CALL
01-240-7200
CREDIT CARD SERVICE
24 HOURS 7 DAYS

Pizza Palace
Newly Opened
FULLY LICENSED TILL MIDNIGHT
7 NIGHTS A WEEK
Serving 130 or more cocktails to
choose from
LIVE MUSIC EVERY FRIDAY
American deep pan pizza's at
their very best!
Eat in West End style at
East End prices
148–150 HIGH ROAD, TOTTENHAM
Tel: 802 2202
⊖ Seven Sisters

Charlie Chan's
Peking & Szechaun Cuisine
Come to Charlie Chan's and
take the mystery out of Chinese cooking.
Charlie Chan's food is always good.
Open Daily noon–3.00pm
6.00pm–midnight
134 Cromwell Road,
Kensington, London SW7
Tel: 370 7617

ARTS THEATRE
Box Office 352000 · Credit Cards 316421
Today 4.30 and 8. Cambridge Theatre Company present.
Henrik Ibsen's
PEER GYNT
"Imaginative production   a rewarding evening" – The Times 5/3/87
30 March–1 April, Alan Ayckbourn's TAKING STEPS
2–4 April, ACCIDENTAL DEATH OF AN ANARCHIST

THEATRES

PART **A**

Before you listen

1) Imagine you are going out for the evening and you can choose to go anywhere from the selection above.
a) Which restaurant/pub would you go to? Why?
b) Would you choose the cinema or the theatre? Which film/play?
c) Would you prefer a classical music concert, the opera or a pop concert?
d) Do you like nightclubs/cocktail bars? What do you think of the one above?

2) With your partner, plan a perfect evening out (money is no problem!).
Remember, you can go to more than one place in the evening. Make notes of how you plan to spend your evening.

Listening activities

3) Listen to Jenny and Nick planning a night out.
On the right is a page from Jenny's diary. Which day does the phone conversation refer to?

4) Listen a second time.
a) Why didn't they see *Castaway*?
   i) Nick knows the film is stupid.
   ii) He didn't like the book.
   iii) Jenny didn't want to.
b) Why didn't they see *Room With A View*?
   i) Nick didn't want to.
   ii) Jenny didn't want to.
   iii) It had finished.
c) Why didn't they see *Colour Of Money*?
   i) Jenny doesn't like Paul Newman.
   ii) Nick didn't want to.
   iii) It wasn't on.
d) Why did they decide to see *Mona Lisa*?
   i) Nick wanted to see it.
   ii) Jenny had never seen it.
   iii) Both of them were happy to see it.

> **JULY 1987**
>
> **MONDAY 13**
> Went to see 'Mona Lisa' at the Arts Brilliant! We went to the pub later and then on to 'Reflections'.
>
> **TUESDAY 14**
> Mum & Dad came round. Cooked them a curry.
>
> **WEDNESDAY 15**
> Saw Nick. We wanted to see 'The Fly' but it was full. Watched T.V.
>
> **THURSDAY 16**
> My birthday, so went to the new nightclub 'Purple Pussy Cat' and on to an Italian restaurant.
>
> **FRIDAY 17**
> Saw Mona Lisa again, with Nick this time. Had a lovely Chinese meal first.
>
> **SATURDAY 18**
> Jane's party. Stayed the night.
>
> **SUNDAY 19**
> 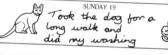 Took the dog for a long walk and did my washing

5) Listen to the dialogue again. Before you listen see if you can remember the exact words used in these situations. Then listen again, and compare.

a) Jenny suggests seeing a film: _____

Nick agrees: _____

Jenny doesn't know what films there are: _____

She asks him to wait (while she gets the paper): _____

b) Nick offers to book seats: _____

He suggests having food first: _____

Jenny agrees: _____

Nick ends the conversation: _____

6) Listen to Nick's words and intonation. How does he:
a) express disappointment (about *Room With A View*) _____
b) express lack of interest (about *Colour Of Money*) _____
c) express enthusiasm (about *Mona Lisa*)? _____

Writing task

Look at Jenny's diary for the week again and then fill in one of your own, for last week.
OR
Ask your partner what he/she did and fill in one for him/her.

UNIT **12**   A Day in the Life of . . .

Before you listen

When you are thinking about choosing a job you will probably think of the following criteria:

- hours
- variety of work
- interesting work
- meeting people
- travel
- holidays
- salary
- career
- other _____
  _____ ?

1) Which are the *three* most important criteria for you? Put a number next to the *three* most important criteria (in order of importance) and discuss your choice with a partner.

2) According to these criteria, discuss which job you would most like, and which job you would *not* like.

PART **B**

Listening activities

3) Listen to three people describing their jobs and write down what you think they do. Write down any vocabulary which helped you to decide.

	JOB?	KEY WORDS
Extract one: Ivy		
Extract two: Heather		
Extract three: Stephen		

4) Listen again, and fill in the following information about each person.
a) Complete this informal job description for Ivy.

Hours: _____
Duties: _____
_____
Advantages of job: _____
_____
Disadvantages of job: _____
_____

b) Imagine that Heather is making notes for a job description. Write down what you think she would say.

Hours: _____
Duties: _____
Personality necessary for job: _____
Advantages: _____
Disadvantages: _____

c) Stephen is making notes to help the community police officer, who is doing his job while he is on holiday. Fill in the blanks with information from the text.

Andy
It's a good idea to go 1_____ before going on patrol so you can liaise. I usually go in around 2_____

On patrol
Remember to always look out for anything 3_____ such as abandoned 4_____
Make sure you go to these places:
a) 5_____ b) Schools c) 6_____
and don't forget to talk to people, in case they have 7_____ or complaints

Traffic regulations
Don't be too strict about parking, seatbelts, etc. Always give a 8_____ the first time. We have to be nice to them.
Good luck! You'll need it! Stephen

5) What do you think Heather (Extract two) means by:
- 'a lot of men feel . . . . . she should be tied to the kitchen sink'

_____

- 'it's not the easiest of situations if you've had a heavy night the night before'

_____

Discuss the answers in groups.

6) Listen to Ivy talking again (Extract one) and make a note of *two* verb forms she uses to express regular habits. Give at least one example of each.

PART C

Writing task

Think of an interesting or unusual job and imagine that you are being interviewed by a magazine about this job. *Do not* say what the job is, but include the following information in your notes. Then write the article for the magazine.
- hours
- likes/dislikes about the job
- what you have to do every day/sometimes
- anything unusual about it

When you have written your article, exchange with a partner, or read it out to your group or class. Your teacher and colleagues will try to guess what job you are describing.

UNIT *13* A Robbery

Do you know this robber?

Photofit of the suspect

hours of the morning and escaped with goods valued at around £2,000. They included items of jewellery, a stereo, a video recorder and a colour TV set. She managed to free herself, unhurt, after he fled. She described him as white, around 5′ 8″, in his late twenties, well-built, clean-shaven, with a pointed nose and straight dark hair.

Two days later a man wearing a stocking mask broke into a factory in the same area and got away with cash of around £3,000. A man fitting the description above was later seen driving away from the scene in an old blue Escort van.

Police are searching for a man who is wanted for questioning about a string of burglaries in the Manchester area, which they suspect may be connected.

In the first of two recent incidents, a man tied up a woman in her own house in the early

Police warn that this man could be armed and therefore dangerous. They have issued the photofit picture above and ask the public to contact them immediately if they have any information.

PART *A*

Before you listen

1) Read the text above and answer the following questions.
a) Why are the police looking for the man in the picture?
b) Who gave the police the description?
c) How old is the man?
d) What was he wearing when he broke into the factory?
e) Why could the man be dangerous?

2) a) Have *you* ever been involved in any kind of robbery?
   b) What different kinds of robberies do you know of?

Listening tasks

3) Listen to Tony talking about an experience he had, and answer the following questions.

- What kind of robbery was it? _____
- Was it a successful robbery? _____
- How did Tony feel a) during it? _____
- b) after it? _____

4) Listen again and fill in the following notes, which the police took during their interview with Tony a few days later.

a) What time of day was it? _____

b) Where was the bank? _____

c) How many customers were in it? _____

d) What was Tony doing when the robbers arrived? _____

e) How many robbers were there? _____

f) What were they wearing? _____

g) What were they carrying? _____

h) What did the robbers say? _____

i) What did people do? _____

j) How did the robbers get the cash? _____

k) What did they say when they left? _____

l) When did the police arrive? _____

m) What did Tony do next? _____

5) Match the words from the text in Column A to their equivalents in Column B. You may need to listen again for the context. One has been done for you.

COLUMN **A**

i) he looked at me *blankly*

ii) absolutely terrifying

iii) deathly hush

iv) a bit panicky

v) I wandered out

vi) I *bumped into* the accountant

vii) absolutely flabbergasted

viii) it only came home to me

ix) disappeared *into thin air*

COLUMN **B**

a) very frightening

b) I realised

c) frightened

d) without any expression

e) walked slowly, casually

f) very, very surprised

g) met by chance

h) complete silence

i) with no indication of where they had gone

Writing task

Using the notes you made in Part B, question 4), write up the report which the police had to make on the robbery.

An Interview with Sir John

PART **A**

Before you listen

This photograph is of Spain's Hall, an old country house near Finchingfield in Essex.

1) Who do you think these people are, and what do you think their relationship is?

2) What kind of lifestyle do you think they have?

Listening activities

3) Listen to the interview.
a) Were your predictions (above) correct?
b) What is the main topic of the interview?

- Sir John's home ☐
- Important guests he has had ☐
- His job ☐

4) Listen again, and answer the following questions.
a) How many people live at Spain's Hall?
b) What are three things a butler has to do?
c) What did Sir John think of Prince Charles?
d) Why did Prince Charles come to Spain's Hall?
e) What was the problem when Princess Margaret came to lunch?
f) Why is conversation with the Royal Family difficult?
g) Why is Bruce surprised by this?
h) What was the problem when Prince Charles came to lunch?
i) How was this solved?

5) a) Sir John says, 'You're not supposed to ask them (the Royal Family) questions'. How else could you say this in English?
b) Sir John says, 'If I'd thought about it, I'd have had dog biscuits.' What do you think he said after the lunch with Princess Margaret?

6) Match the words in Column A (from the text) with their equivalents in Column B. You may need to listen again for the context.

COLUMN **A**

i) bachelor ☐
ii) astonished ☐
iii) delightful ☐
iv) fixed up ☐
v) wolfed it ☐

COLUMN **B**

a) ate it quickly
b) very nice
c) unmarried man
d) very surprised
e) prepared

PART **C**

Writing task

Imagine you are a friend of Sir John's and you are helping him to prepare for a dinner party he is having for Prince Charles and Princess Diana.
- Write the menu you think you should serve.
- Make a list of possible topics of conversation (also those to avoid!) for your other guests, so that there will be no embarrassing situations, yet enough to talk about.

This Proud Land

in this proud land we grew up strong
2 we were wanted all along
I was taught to fight, taught to win
4 I never thought I could fail

no fight left or so it seems
6 I am a man whose dreams have all deserted
I've changed my face, I've changed my name
8 but no one wants you when you lose

though I saw it all around
10 never thought that I could be affected
thought that we'd be last to go
12 it is so strange the way things turn

PART **A**

Before you listen

1) Read the text above, which is the first part of a song by Peter Gabriel and try to answer the following questions:
a) What do you think has happened to this man?
b) Think of some adjectives to describe how he feels.
c) What kind of childhood do you think he had, and why is this important? What words does he use to suggest this?
d) Why do you think he uses the expression 'proud land'?
e) What do you think 'it' refers to in line 9?

2) The next verse of the song (below) is mixed up. In what order do you think the lines come? Write numbers 1–4 next to the appropriate line.

a) as daylight broke, I saw the earth   ☐

b) drove the night toward my home   ☐

c) the place that I was born, on the lakeside   ☐

d) the trees had burned down to the ground   ☐

3) What does this verse tell us about how the man feels? Why is there a reference to the 'burned trees'?

PART **B**

Listening activities

4) Listen to the first half of the song once and check if you ordered the verse correctly.
a) What do you think the relationship is between the man and the woman?
b) What advice is she giving him?

5) Listen to the second part of the song and decide what the song might be about and what the title is. Have you changed your mind about question 1) e)?

6) Listen to the second part of the song again and fill in the gaps.

got to [1]_____ out of here

I can't [2]_____ any more

going to [3]_____ on that [4]_____

keep my [5]_____ down below

[6]_____ may come

and [7]_____ may go

that [8]_____'s flowing

that [9]_____'s flowing

[10]_____ on to another [11]_____

tried hard to settle [12]_____

for every [13]_____ so many men

so many men no one [14]_____

7) In the song you will notice that a lot of phrasal verbs are used.

- grew up
- burned down
- move on
- give up
- fall back
- settle down

Listen again to the song, or look carefully at the context (in the tapescript) to see if you can work out the meaning of these expressions, and then try to complete the following sentences with the most appropriate expression taken from the list above.

a) The firemen got to the house as quickly as they could, but unfortunately it had already _____ _____ .

b) I live in London now, but I _____ _____ in Manchester.

c) As soon as I reached the age of thirty, everyone told me I should buy a house or get married and _____ _____ instead of travelling around the world.

d) After I failed my driving test three times I _____ _____ and bought a bicycle instead.

e) When I am reading a foreign language I try not to worry about all the new words I don't know, but I often _____ _____ on my dictionary.

f) I worked in the same place for twenty years but then I realised it was time to _____ _____ if I wanted more money.

PART C

Writing task

Imagine you are a friend of the woman or the man in the song. Write a letter giving advice on what to do.
OR
Write a poem or essay on the subject of unemployment, or another issue which is of importance in your country.

The Supernatural

Before you listen

1) Which of the following statements do you believe? Write down a number between 1 and 5 next to each statement, depending on how strongly you feel for/ against it (5 = strongly in favour, 1 = not at all in favour).

a) Sometimes inanimate objects move without human help – probably with the help of spirits. ☐

b) Some people can predict the future by reading cards, looking into a crystal ball, examining your teacup, etc. ☐

c) People's characters are, to some extent, formed by the stars. ☐

d) It is sometimes possible to read other people's minds, without speaking to them. ☐

e) You can learn to tell someone's character by studying their handwriting. ☐

f) If you break a mirror, seven years bad luck will follow. ☐

g) Sometimes the spirit of a dead person can return to haunt a person or a place. ☐

h) You can predict someone's future by studying their hands. ☐

2) Discuss your beliefs and any past experiences, in groups.

3) Match the statements above with one of the words below. The first one is done for you.

a) Superstition ｜f｜   e) Poltergeists ☐

b) Palmistry ☐   f) Telepathy ☐

c) Astrology ☐   g) Fortune telling ☐

d) Ghosts ☐   h) Graphology ☐

Listening activities

4) Listen once to the text.
a) Decide which of the topics above they are talking about.
b) Decide whether you agree most with Paul, Karen or Bruce.

5) Listen to the text again and decide who puts forward the following ideas. Tick (✔) the appropriate box.

	PAUL	KAREN	BRUCE
a) If ghosts do exist they will probably appear in old places.			
b) The fact that so many people have seen ghosts means you should believe these people.		✔	

	PAUL	KAREN	BRUCE
c) It doesn't mean ghosts don't exist just because you haven't seen one.			✓
d) Some people prefer to think ghosts exist to add more excitement and 'colour' to life.	✓		
e) People used to believe in the supernatural because there was no scientific explanation at the time for strange things.			
f) Some people start out by not believing in ghosts and then change their minds.			✓
g) Some people don't believe in the supernatural because they won't admit that there are things which the 'rational mind' can't explain.		✓	

6) Match the italic words or phrases (taken from the text) to their equivalents below. The first one is done for you.

a) 'Oh some *daft* article about a haunted house'
b) 'I don't think that we've got any *proof* that they don't exist'
c) 'I think it's a bit *narrow-minded* of you to say that there's no such thing'
d) 'I've had no *evidence* and until I do I shan't believe in it'
e) 'I would never *scoff* the idea'
f) 'I would never turn round and say it's a *load of rubbish*'
g) 'people want to believe in ghosts because their lives are so *tedious* that they invent stories'
h) 'I am *convinced* there are times when you've got to believe them'
i) 'they *turn out* to be believers'

g	i) boring		vi) speak with contempt (as if the idea is stupid)
	ii) something that gives a reason for believing something		vii) something that gives a reason for believing something
	iii) stupid/silly		viii) they finish
	iv) very sure		ix) unable to accept other people's ideas
	v) nonsense/worthless		

PART C

Writing task

A friend of yours is doing research on superstitions in countries around the world. She has discovered, for example, that in Britain the number 13 is considered unlucky and that walking under a ladder will also bring bad luck. On the other hand, a horseshoe is supposed to bring good luck.

Write a list for your friend (Sarah) with as many superstitions as you can think of from your country, and add a note to her saying which ones *you* believe.

Disaster

PART **A**

Before you listen

1) Look at the picture above.
a) What has happened?
b) In what part of the world do you think it is?
c) How do you think the people feel?
d) What do you think they will do next?

Listening activities

2) Listen to the news on the radio.
a) What is the main news? earthquake
b) Where and when did these events take place?
c) Can you remember one more headline?

3) Try to complete the following report which appeared in the newspaper the same day. Then listen again to check your answers.

EARTHQUAKE PANIC

[1] Tremors were felt all over southern Italy last night as the country was shaken by a massive earthquake in the south of the country. More than [2] 400 people are thought to have [3] died. [4] hundreds of buildings have been destroyed in Naples itself and there has been devastation in isolated [5] _____ outside the city. [6] telephone lines have been broken and [7] _____ operations are being delayed because of the dreadful [8] _____ conditions and the poor road connections. Tear gas was used when panic broke out in the [9] prison and there is chaos on the roads as people leave the city and [10] _____ for the countryside.

4) a) Look at the text again and underline every time the <u>passive</u> is used.
   Example: Tremors <u>were felt</u> . . .
   Find six more examples in the text of different forms of the passive.
   b) Discuss *how* the passive is formed and *when* we use it in English.

Writing task

Imagine you are the correspondent who is at the disaster area. Write an imaginary dialogue between you and one of the survivors, to be sent back to your newspaper.

Remembering My Schooldays

Tim Moores went to Harrow, one of the most famous public schools in Britain, in the 1950s. He was sent there at the age of twelve and ran away four years later.

PART **A**

Before you listen

1) Look at the photograph (above) of Harrow, and some of its students, and discuss the following questions.

a) What kind of school do you think it is? (a day school/boarding school? comfortable?)

b) What kind of people do you think go there? (what do you think is more important for those people – social class, intelligence, wealth?)

c) What advantages do you think there are of going to a school like this?

d) What disadvantages do you think there might be?

Listening activities

2) Listen to the text once and discuss with your teacher to what extent your predictions were correct, and what (if anything) surprised you?

3) What is the main aim of the school? Tick the appropriate box.

a) to produce academics ☐

b) to produce sportsmen ☐

c) to produce 'gentlemen' ☐

4) What do you think the headmaster would regard as the important qualities of a 'Harrovian' in Tim's time? Tick the appropriate boxes.
Did you need to . . . ?

- be an individual ☐   • be good at sport ☐

- work hard ☐   • be well-dressed/elegant ☐

- be 'masculine' ☐   • be clever ☐

- mix well with other boys ☐   • be able to lead/influence others ☐

- conform ☐

5) Which *two* qualities do you think would be the most important for a Harrovian – for example, if you were choosing a headboy at Harrow? Give evidence from the text.

6) Which of these 'ideal' qualities do you think Tim did *not* have? You will have to 'read between the lines' here.

7) Use the words in the list below (taken from the text) to complete the following summary.

team	swot	pain
dropped	tough	hard
overcoat	hero	frowned on

If you were clever you would be called a [1]_____, whereas if you were good at games (or, at least, [2]_____ games) you were thought of as a [3]_____ . Other games, such as tennis and golf were [4]_____ _____ .

You never complained about [5]_____ or discomfort because, if you were a 'real gentleman' you had to be [6]_____ and [7]_____ . This is also the reason why you didn't wear an [8]_____ even if the temperature [9]_____ below freezing.

Writing task

Imagine you are Tim writing to his headmaster to give his reasons why he ran away from school. Write the note he left behind when he went, suggesting improvements which could be made at the school.

Radio Phone-In

The legal problem page
'THE LAW AND YOU'

A

The other weekend I bought a jacket for my son in a sale. When I got home he said it was too small and refused to wear it so I went back the next day and asked them to exchange it for a larger size. Unfortunately they didn't have a larger size and when I asked for my money back they refused, saying that no refunds were given on sales goods. Are they within their rights to do this?
Annoyed

B

Myself and two friends have been renting a house near the college we go to for the last two years. The landlord has now decided he wants us to leave and has more or less said that we have to be out within the next two weeks. We have nowhere else to go and with exams coming up shortly we would rather stay where we are. Friends of ours are saying he can't get us out unless we have signed a contract agreeing to go. Is this right?
Worried

C

I have been living in what used to be a very quiet area for about a year now but in the last few months it has changed completely – if I had known this would happen I would never have bought my house. Opposite me there is now a fish and chip shop which fries day and night except for Sunday – the smell is disgusting and so are all the empty paper bags all over the street. It doesn't close until after midnight so every night there are people shouting, radios blaring, car doors slamming – I never seem to get a night's sleep these days and it's beginning to affect my work. Is there anything I can do?
Exhausted

PART *A*

Before you listen

1) Look at the letters above from a weekly magazine. What do you think the answers will be?

A a) They must give you your money back, or a credit note. ☐

   b) They are not obliged to do anything. ☐

B a) He can get you out if he needs the house back for his family. ☐

   b) Your friends are right. ☐

C a) There is nothing you can do except move. ☐

   b) If the disturbance happens regularly you can ask a solicitor to write to them. ☐

Discuss your answers in groups.

Listening activities

2) Listen to a legal expert, Charles Andrews, talking and match the caller with his or her letter. Put a circle round the appropriate letter below.

First caller: A   B   C

Second caller: A   B   C

3) Complete the following summaries, using the words listed below each summary.

a) Shops are not legally ^{1}_____ to give you your money back or

^{2}_____ goods if the items are bought in a ^{3}_____

although most big stores would probably give you a

^{4}_____ _____ if you had a ^{5}_____ .

> receipt   sale   credit note   obliged   exchange

b) Stephen has not ^{1}_____ an agreement but he pays

^{2}_____ monthly. The ^{3}_____ does not live in the house

and ^{4}_____ no services. He has to write formally asking them to

leave – at least a ^{5}_____ in advance. Unless he wants the house for

himself or ^{6}_____ _____ , Stephen is probably a

protected ^{7}_____ .

> month   rent   provides   landlord   tenant   his   family   signed

Writing tasks

Write a letter of reply to 'Exhausted', suggesting what she might do. Use expressions like:
- if I were you
- why don't you
- you should
- have you thought about _____ ing?

Places I Know

Before you listen

1) Think about the town or village that you live in now, or the place where you were born, and think of three things you *like* about it and three things that you *dislike*.

LIKE

1 _____

2 _____

3 _____

DISLIKE

1 _____

2 _____

3 _____

2) How would you change it if you could? Write down at least two suggestions.

1 _____

2 _____

Listening activities

3) Listen to three people talking about places they know, and make a list of the things they like and dislike about them.

	LIKES	DISLIKES
Extract one: Pat		
Extract two: David		
Extract three: Cindy		

4) Listen again, and answer the following questions.

Extract one
a) How often does Pat visit her friends in France?
b) How big is the village where they live?
c) What was their house before they modernised it?
d) How do they spend their time there?
e) What presents can you buy in the village?

Extract two
a) How old are most of the buildings in Tokyo?
b) Why are most of the buildings not high?
c) How do you get on the trains in the busy periods?
d) Why is it a problem to go to the public gardens?
e) How big is Tokyo?

Extract three
a) Is the town unusual in any way?
b) Is it a poor place?
c) How does she feel about being a child there?
d) How did she feel about leaving?
e) How do you avoid the cold?

Writing task

Imagine you have been asked to write an advertisement to 'sell' your home town, or another place you know. First make a list of all the good things about living there and then design an advert based on the one below.

OR

Write an extract for a guidebook about your home town.

Tapescript

UNIT 1   A New Job

Operator: Hello, Woolworths'.
Sue: Ah hello. I wonder if I could speak to the Personnel Manager, please?
Operator: Yes, certainly. If you'll hold on a minute I'll put you through.
Sue: Thank you.
John: Hello, John Adams speaking.
Sue: Ah good morning, Mr Adams, er I saw your advertisement in the Saffron Walden Reporter for a hostess (Oh yes) and I wondered if you could give me a few more details about the job.
John: Yes, certainly. Er perhaps I should make it clear from the start it is, it is a part time job. (Ah) Er yes we would need you from ten in the morning until two in the afternoon, roughly.
Sue: Yes, yes, I didn't realise that, actually. It wasn't clear in the advertisement.
John: Aha. Are you, are you still interested?
Sue: Well I am interested, but it would depend to some extent on what the salary is.
John: Yes, well we're offering about £75 a week (Yes) erm obviously this may be a little bit more if you have the right qualifications and experience. (Mmm) Have you in fact had any experience in catering?
Sue: Well, yes, I have. Er, I'm at present working for and have been working for the same firm for about five years, for a small firm of er consultant engineers (Mm yeah) and I've been doing work rather similar to the kind of work that I think er is described in the advertisement.
John: Yes, well, I mean we have a fairly small staff here, we're talking about fifteen to twenty people (Yes) so your duties will be sort of to prepare and serve the food at just at lunchtimes.
Sue: I see. Yes, I'm sure I'd be able to manage that – that wouldn't be a problem.
John: Yes well erm that sounds about right. Er perhaps you could come down for an interview some time?
Sue: Yes, yes, when would be suitable for you?
John: Er let me just have a look at my diary. Er yes, perhaps, what about, what about next Wednesday at about 2.30 in the afternoon? Would that be all right for you?
Sue: Wednesday er 2.30. Yes, that, I think that would be fine, actually. That's OK.
John: Ah good. Yeah, and perhaps you could bring any qualifications you've got so we could have a look at them and er . . .
Sue: Yes, yes, OK.
John: Could you just tell me who you're working for at the moment?
Sue: I'm working for, er, Bloggses actually in the High Street.
John: Right, OK and could I just have your name?
Sue: Yes er my name, my surname is Boardman. That's BOARDMAN (Yeah) and my initial is S.
John: Right, OK, S Boardman (Yes) OK OK Miss Boardman. Well, see you then next Wednesday at 2.30.
Sue: OK. Thanks very much then.
John: Lovely. OK. Bye.
Sue: Bye.

UNIT 2   Julia's Strange Experience (1)

The night of Julia's strange encounter was wild and stormy. The rain beat against her windscreen and the trees swayed in the wind as she drove home. There was no moon to lighten the lonely country lane but occasional flashes of lightning lit up the sea far below, the waves crashing against the cliffs. Julia turned up the music on her stereo and wished she hadn't decided to drive back from the party on her own.

It had been well after midnight when she left but the other guests had shown no signs of leaving. She had decided to go even though she had no very clear idea of the way home. It was the first time she had been to this friend's house and now she was beginning to think she had taken a wrong turning. She was afraid she was lost.

Suddenly she slammed her foot on the brake; there was a large, black object in the middle of the road blocking her way. She stopped just in time and saw two green eyes staring back at her, reflecting the beam of her headlights. Julia realised it was the largest cat she had ever seen. It just sat there, looking straight at her. What on earth was it doing in the middle of the road and in a thunderstorm in the pouring rain in the middle of nowhere? Perhaps it was injured?

Julia switched off the engine and picked up her torch. She got out and went up to the cat but just as she shone her torch on it the cat miaowed, stretched and walked off into the trees. Julia was both puzzled and annoyed as she got back into the car. She was wet through, though she'd only been out a few seconds. Oh well, she thought, at least I'm not completely alone on this road.

She turned the key in the ignition. Nothing. The engine would not start. She tried again and again but the engine was completely dead. Julia shivered. She was cold and wet but she was also beginning to panic. She wondered what to do. Should she try to find a phone box? No, there didn't seem to be any sign of civilisation near here, and besides, she would probably catch pneumonia if she went out into the rain again.

She sat in the dark, listening to the rain drumming on the roof. She couldn't even listen to the radio now. She wrapped her coat round her and settled down to wait for morning. Gradually she calmed down and began to feel sleepy. The rain went on and on.

Suddenly she sat up, wide awake. She realised the rain had stopped. She could only hear the beating of her heart. Why was she so afraid? Then she heard it. Someone was opening the passenger door. Julia screamed!

UNIT 3   Snakes and Other Animals

Interviewer: Mr Mercer, what is your job exactly?
Vet: I'm a veterinary surgeon in general practice, looking after all different sorts of animals – sheep, goats, pigs, horses, dogs, cats – we do have some lions and tigers at the zoo er we have a few bears, wolves, otters – you name it we look after it.
Interviewer: What sort of pets do people bring you here to your surgery mainly?
Vet: Well, mostly it's going to be dogs and cats but then we have snakes and parrots and rats and ferrets and all the other animals that people keep as pets.
Interviewer: You mention snakes – why do you think

people keep snakes? What's the attraction in that?

Vet: Well, I quite like snakes but I wouldn't actually want one as a pet erm I think they keep them to frighten other people with really. No, some people are very keen on snakes, they like having them.

Interviewer: What do you find attractive about snakes?

Vet: They're all muscle, they're not sort of slimy, as people think, they're all muscle, fairly powerful. We do have some problems. One or two of the smaller ones will snap at you but in general it's the big crushing snakes that we deal with. We had one in here one day that was thirteen foot long – took three of us to lift it. Now if that gets round you twice, wrapped round you a couple of times, then you really are in for a good hug.

Interviewer: Now the British people have a reputation for being very animal-minded. Do you think the British spend more money on their animals than their children?

Vet: It depends on the people. Some people are very good with their animals, some people are reasonable with their animals erm, some go absolutely over the top and treat them far better than they would their children, and unfortunately there are a group of people that are cruel to their animals and so we do a certain amount of work with the Royal – RSPCA.

Interviewer: What experience have you had of people who treat their animals too well?

Vet: Lots of animals come in for surgery with lipstick marks on their head – we regard that as a specific sort of condition here and we always make a comment on it.

Interviewer: Do you think animals are good for people's health?

Vet: Well, of late we now talk about companion animals rather than pets and certainly people are taking dogs and cats into hospitals, to old people's homes where a social contact is needed and this sort of patting of animals seems to help old people, and certainly we have old people who have budgerigars and other small animals and they're very much their life – they maybe see one person every two days but their animal is with them all the time, and it's a companion.

Interviewer: Do animals ever attack you when you're handling them?

Vet: Mostly we handle them very easily, it's only occasionally that we get hurt by animals, scratched and bitten by cats, bitten by dogs and my partner recently got very badly hurt by a horse – so we have a dangerous job as well as an enjoyable job.

I think probably the thing I like best about it is delivering new animals. It never fails to amaze me how one moment you can have one mother and the next moment you can have a pile of animals and, I think the day I don't get pleasure out of delivering new born animals I shall give up.

Interviewer: But you're still very much interested in your job?

Vet: Oh love it, love it. I would like a lot less paperwork, and I'd like just to do veterinary medicine, but unfortunately you take on a sort of package.

Interviewer: OK. Thank you very much indeed.

UNIT 4 Street life

Extract one

Peter: In my particular group of cottages the walls are only one brick thick and one is aware of one's neighbours at various times of the day – in fact this last week has been a very very difficult with one particular group of neighbours, both of which are – one is well over eighty and one is coming up to eighty and they've been on at each other the whole, almost continually the whole week. They've been arguing, the fact that one is stone deaf means the other one is shrieking at the top of her voice which . . . The other problem is that the neighbour opposite tends to be a little bit of a nightbird so that, and he can't live without music, which means that up to sometimes up to two and three o'clock in the morning I can hear the bass of his stereo which he insists is not to him very loud but to me it's just like a Chinese water torture.

Extract two

Peter: Every house in this, almost every house in this lane has one, two, three or more cats, and to be woken up at half past four in the morning with two cats fighting under one's bedroom window is not something I find pleasant.

Helen: Well I find that cat owners have a sort of law unto themselves. It's perfectly all right for their cat to come into your garden, but if I let my little dog into someone's garden to poop and make messes all over the place I think they'd go berserk and quite honestly I encourage my dog to chase cats in our garden because they really do cause a lot of damage.

Extract three

Helen: Well, I think they're really first buyers' cottages or old people's cottages, and people on their own, yes they're all sort of the same type of people.

Peter: Well, no, I don't agree, I don't agree wholly there, Helen, erm I mean if you look at our particular group here you've got Mrs Lawson who is, she's in her eighties and then you've got Tim, next-door but one, who is a film director, and Robert, who is a thatcher, with his Italian girlfriend, we're not really all the same.

we're all independent go-getting people as opposed to sort of boring sort of nine to five job-type people.

Peter: Oh well, yes, I suppose I agree with you there, as far as the nine till five but I mean there's a tremendous variety in ages I think in the lane, and I think probably the older people benefit this, in the fact that they are well looked after.

Extract four

Peter: One of the good things about living in a close community is that there is no need to worry about locking your front door or your car doors when you go to the shops or you go to visit friends. It's like living in a shop window, completely. Everything is noticed, it's part of the thing to see who's in and out of the lane so that if a stranger does come everybody is on the notice you know to see what's happening so that you can be quite safe about at the moment, leaving the house.

Extract five

Peter: And then there was the time that I was woken up in the middle of the night by my next-door neighbour whose ex-husband had arrived asking to see his daughter, and the fact that he was blind drunk didn't help. He refused to go away and was shouting very loudly so the police was called by another neighbour and they arrived about two o'clock, so you had the father shouting, the next-door neighbour opposite shouting at him and the police arriving with blue lights flashing. Oh yes, there's never a dull moment living in the lane.

Tapescript

UNIT 5 My kind of sport

a) Jo

Well, I've been playing it since I was at school – since I was quite young, 'cos my dad was always very keen on it and he used to give me lessons, and then at university I joined a team and we used to play quite a lot.

It's quite fashionable at the moment, actually, all over Europe it's becoming more fashionable and it's often difficult to book courts, you've got to get in there a week before. Um I like it because it requires a lot of stamina, you've got to be fit, it's constant running right the way through and it doesn't take a long time. You can take off an hour at lunchtime, go off, play, have a shower, come back and it's all over with, and you've done a lot and it's not a lot of standing around, it's movement all the time.

Er, you're often absolutely exhausted at the end, and you can't really play for two hours at a shot although some people do. It's usually for quite a short time.

b) Brian

I think I've been playing now for nearly forty years, ever since I was a little kid on the beach at Blackpool, and it's always been my great passion in life.

When I watch a game I appreciate the athletic skill of the players, the tactics of the manager or coach, and the thrill of the uncertainty, just not knowing how the game's going to go, even when a very strong team's playing a very weak team. There's always that possibility of a surprise, of the unexpected moment changing the game.

c) Stephanie

Well, I've been doing it every winter holiday since I can remember. I love doing it because it's a skill that improves every time you do it, er it's fast and it's exhilarating and although it's really cold you can still get a tan when you do it. Of course the scenery's beautiful and it's really nice when you're tired to go and have a drink in a bar afterwards. Of course the problem is that it's expensive – you have to buy the equipment; the instruction's expensive too and it's really dangerous, you can always break a leg doing it, but apart from that, I really like it.

UNIT 6 Holiday plans

Alistair: Well, I'm off tomorrow I'm leaving tomorrow, great, holiday (Oh really), yes.
Barbara: Oh, nice, where are you going?
Alistair: Italy.
Mike: Tell us more.
Alistair: Well I'm leaving at eight tomorrow morning (From here?). Yes, driving to Gatwick, so that's about an hour, er so I'm arriving at the airport 9 o'clock and taking off 10 o'clock. Er going on a cultural holiday, this is what I've wanted to do for a long time (Yes). The usual sort of thing is lying on a beach but this is going to be a bit different.
Barbara: Yes, you don't you don't like that do you?
Alistair: No, no, so I'm hoping to do some museums, art galleries, taste a bit of the food and the drink and the lifestyle of Italy, I've always wanted to go there. There are, I've got I've got a whole list of you know museums and art galleries and in fact I'm hiring a car in Milan so I can drive around a bit. I can leave Milan and go south if I get bored with that city, so I'm really looking forward to it.
Barbara: Well that's not really my cup of tea at all for a

holiday. No I don't think I'll be doing that this year.
Mike: What are your plans then Barbara?
Barbara: Well, I'm not sure. I may go somewhere, well I don't know, I may go to Tenerife, I just want something, you know, where I can just relax, lie in the sun for two weeks and come back, you know, looking fantastic, but I'm not sure where I'm going to go. I might go to Tenerife, might go to Greece, you know, I haven't really made up my mind.
Alistair: So you're not a culture vulture like myself?
Barbara: Oh no, no, I mean I like watching programmes on the television, you know, but when it comes to walking round museums for your holiday no, no, that's not me at all. I'm far happier, you know, drinking up the old sunshine on the beach there.
Mike: Yes. I agree about that, actually.
Barbara: Dropping into a bar at you know lunchtime, back on the beach. What about you, Mike? What's your plans?
Mike: Well I'm quite happy to stay in England.
Barbara: Really? (Yes) Oh what about the weather?
Mike: Weather's no problem (A brave man!) I'll take it as it comes, yes sure. No, I shall head off north to the Lake District as I usually do. I'm going at the end of term (Nice). I've got a week free (Have you got something booked?). Yes (What sort of thing?) Small cottage (Nice), self-catering, like to do that, don't trust anybody else's food (No) so I shall do that. (And what you'll be going out every day, walking?) Right, that's the routine.
Barbara: But what about if it's really raining, or . . . ?
Mike: Well, if it's raining really hard, if it's really chucking it down I'll go out in the car, perhaps, but I really don't mind, I really don't mind going out in bad weather.
Barbara: But you go out rain or shine?
Mike: I don't mind, yes, no, I've got the equipment, I don't mind, in fact it's often more exciting if the weather's a bit wild.
Alistair: Wind, rain, all that business.
Mike: The elements you know.
Barbara: Well, I wish you luck, it's not my scene at all.
Alistair: Nor mine I'm afraid, no.

UNIT 7 Frightening experiences

Jan: Brian, you've had some fairly horrifying experiences in your life, haven't you? I mean, having lived all over the world and things like that.
Brian: Yes, I've been in earthquakes, hurricanes, tornados, seen tidal waves, volcanos erupting, just about everything – all possible – floods, all possible natural disasters, but I think the most frightening experience was being involved in a bus crash.
Jan: In this country?
Brian: No, this was in Africa, in a bus which was going through the countryside on a dirt road. Er it was a bus crowded with people, crowded with luggage and the bus had stopped at a small town, at a bar, where the driver had a few beers and then loaded a crate of beer on the bus on the roofrack. When we eventually set off from that place the driver got up speed and suddenly ran off the road. Er, I remember the bus turning over two or three times and of grabbing hold of a handle and eventually the bus came to rest upside down. All I could feel was a tremendous bang on the head which later turned out to be the crate of beer. The

only sound was of the engine still running.

Jan: People weren't screaming, and things like that?

Brian: No, there was a dead silence, absolute shocked silence and it was a long way from any town or any village and the only thing you could hear was the engine. The driver ran away into the bush, he was frightened, so what happened was everybody crawled out through the back window and left their suitcases and possessions and everyone was terrified the bus would explode and eventually someone had the sense to turn the engine off and we all crawled back in again to get our possessions, and no one seemed particularly injured, everyone was just shocked and stunned and it was only after about ten or fifteen minutes of sitting on the ground that people began to collapse and become unconscious and suddenly appear very seriously injured. Eventually a lorry came and took us to hospital and it was only in hospital I realised just how serious it was. A girl sitting next to me on the bus was also sitting next to me in the hospital and the nurse was asking her her age, her religion, etc. etc., and suddenly the girl just lay down and died, and three other people who'd been sitting near me also died.

So I think even though I've been in earthquakes and floods, that was the most frightening experience, being in the bus as it turned over and over.

UNIT 8 Are You a Good Language Learner?

The topic I'd like to deal with this morning is what makes a good language learner. This is an eternal problem, and one to which there's no real solution. I would however like you to think about the situation of learners outside the classroom because in many ways it would be true to say that there are more people in the world who speak a foreign language or a second language who didn't learn it in a classroom than there are who did and I think this awareness of the success of out-of-classroom learning provides us with a key to how *in*-classroom learning can be successful.

Let us look then at the characteristics of a good language learner. I think motivation is certainly going to be very high on our list. Obviously there are different kinds of motivation; there is what we call instrumental motivation, this is the kind of motivation which in theory persuades a school pupil to learn a language in order to pass an examination – it's external motivation, something which is imposed on the learner. The opposite of this is integrative motivation, the kind of motivation which gets an immigrant in a country or someone who's married to a speaker of another language to master the tongue much more rapidly than someone learning in a classroom. Arguably most people possess mixed motivation although it would appear from research that integrative motivation does give much better results, certainly as far as speed of learning goes.

Personality is obviously another major factor to be borne in mind – not necessarily, I'm not necessarily saying that you need – er how shall I say? – extroverts to learn a foreign language, but someone who has the confidence to make mistakes is always going to learn much more quickly than someone who is afraid to experiment.

Intelligence isn't a factor, I feel, in language learning – I would prefer to use the term learning skills. Learning skills are those abilities which make one person progress at a much faster speed than the others; they include having a good ear, efficient revision, being able to monitor your own speech, suitable organisation of learning generally.

However, if we go back to our starting point, which was the great, the much greater number of speakers of languages who have learnt outside classrooms I think it gives us the key to what I believe is the most important factor, and that's independence. A learner who frees him or herself from the tyranny of the teacher and the classroom and who makes use of twenty-four hours a day for learning, who, in a word, accepts responsibility for learning, is always going to be not just a good language learner but the best. Conversely, someone who won't accept this responsibility is always going to remain at what we call a plateau – they've failed to make progress and blame their teachers. In reality it is themselves that they should blame.

UNIT 9 Children Talking

Bruce: Right now, Simon, how much pocket money do you get?

Simon: £4.

Bruce: What do you spend it on?

Simon: Computer games. Things like pencils, pens, sweets. I buy cars and things like those, and footballs.

Bruce: And how much money do you get, Louisa?

Louisa: I get a £1 a week.

Bruce: Ah not so much.

Louisa: No.

Bruce: And what do you spend it on?

Louisa: Tapes and other things, records, and anything musical, really.

Bruce: So you spend a lot of time listening to music?

Louisa: Yes.

Bruce: So what do you do in your spare time?

Louisa: Well, I clean out my guinea pig and play with her, and I play with the dogs and I swim and I play tennis and I play football with my younger brother.

Bruce: What about you, Simon. What do you do after school?

Simon: Well in the weekends I go to football training, I do the odd sport, I play on my computer, I watch the odd occasional television programme, I listen to the odd music . . . odd piece of music, things like that.

Bruce: How much television do you watch?

Simon: Quite a lot, I'm a kind of tele-addict.

Bruce: Do your parents allow you to stay up when you want?

Simon: No. I have to go to bed very very early when it's on weekdays and when, on the weekends I'm allowed to go to bed quite late, about – the latest I'd be allowed to go up is about ten o'clock.

Bruce: And during the week what time do you go to bed?

Simon: About 8.

Bruce: Are your parents strict in any other ways?

Simon: Yes. (In what ways?) They make me eat all the food, and the stuff which I don't like. I don't like any vegetables, and I have to eat them, and other things, like I'm not allowed to play football in the back garden, 'cos I broke a window once, and I'm not allowed to leave my toys in the lounge and kitchen, only in my bedroom, and the playroom.

Bruce: What about you, Louisa – do you have strict parents?

Louisa: Well, I was sort of born to like brown bread and

Tapescript

brown rice. I mean, Mummy's always getting us all these good things and she hates sort of white bread and she's quite strict about that. She's strict about us going to bed – we go to bed at 8 o'clock and then we have our light out at half past 8.

Bruce: OK, Simon, have you ever been on holiday abroad?

Simon: Yes. Austria, and er other places. We go to Austria every year, um, since I was about . . . since I was about two actually they've taken me to Austria because my mum's Austrian and she's got all of her family over in Austria.

Bruce: Louisa, have you ever been abroad?

Louisa: I normally go once a year, but to nowhere special, normally we go on skiing holidays with friends but we've been to Portugal, France and Italy and other places. I like going abroad because you find different places and you see how other people sort of live.

UNIT 10   Julia's Strange Experience (2)

'Are you lost?' said a gentle voice. Julia was too frightened to speak. A woman had opened the door of the car and was leaning in, looking at her kindly. She looked as if she was in her forties, with long black hair and large, rather sad eyes. She was wearing a long blue overcoat – rather old-fashioned, Julia thought – with a bright red scarf wrapped tightly round her neck. Her hair and clothes were soaking wet, but Julia noticed that the rain had almost stopped, though the wind was still strong. The sky had cleared, and now the full moon shone down brightly.

'Are you alright?', the woman said again.

'Oh yes, thank you,' Julia stammered. 'But my car won't start. Do you know if there's a phonebox near here?'

'Well', said the woman, 'I'll take you to a house and you can phone from there.' Without waiting for an answer she set off ahead and Julia had to run to catch her up. The woman walked fast and said very little. After a few minutes they came round a corner and saw a small cottage hidden in some trees. The woman walked straight up to the front door and knocked loudly. The house was quiet and dark. She knocked again and this time a light went on upstairs. Julia heard someone coming down the stairs and then the door was opened slowly by a grey-haired man in a dressing gown.

'Yes?' he said, 'What do you want at this time of night?'

Julia waited for the woman to speak but suddenly she realised that the woman was not there. She must have walked off quietly as they were waiting for the man to open the door.

'Oh, er, my car's broken down. I'm sorry to wake you up but you see . . .' Julia didn't know quite what to say.

'Come in, come in', said the old man. 'It's not a night to be out in'. As he spoke, Julia noticed that he was looking over her shoulder out into the night. It was as if he was expecting someone else. Julia went in.

'There's no point in phoning anyone now,' he said, before she could speak. 'It's four in the morning and besides, you look exhausted. You can sleep in the spare bedroom.'

Upstairs in the room the man opened a wardrobe and pulled out a nightgown. 'These are my wife's clothes,' he said 'but they should fit you.' As he closed the wardrobe, Julia glimpsed a bright red scarf hanging up. When he had left her, Julia opened the wardrobe again. Yes, there was the scarf hanging neatly over the shoulders of a long blue overcoat. Julia reached out her hand and touched them. They were wet. How strange, Julia thought. Just then she saw a photograph standing on the bedside table. It was a picture of a woman. She was about forty, with long dark hair and large sad eyes.

'It's her!' thought Julia. 'She must be his daughter. But where did she go and how did she manage to put her coat and scarf away?' Julia was too tired to think anymore. She got into bed and fell asleep.

When she woke up the sun was shining, and looking out of the window she could see the sea was calm after the storm. Downstairs, in the kitchen the old man was alone, making coffee.

'Morning,' he said, 'Sit down and have some breakfast.'

'Thank you,' said Julia. 'I suppose it was your daughter who brought me here last night.'

'My daughter?' said the man. 'No, I don't have any children.'

'Then who's that in the photo upstairs?' said Julia.

'Ah,' said the man, suddenly looking very sad. 'That was my wife, God bless her. She disappeared twenty years ago. It was a stormy night just like last night; she never came back. She must have slipped off the cliffs and drowned but we never found the body. If only she hadn't gone out to look for William – I knew he'd be alright, though he was only small then.'

'William?' whispered Julia.

'Ah, here he comes now,' said the old man. The kitchen door swung open and in walked an enormous black cat. It looked up at her, and Julia knew she had seen those green eyes before.

UNIT 11   A Night Out

Nick: Hi Jenny.

Jenny: Oh hi Nick. How are you?

Nick: Not so bad. What about this evening then?

Jenny: You mean going out (Yeah). Oh I dunno, I'm feeling a bit tired. I mean, maybe if we went – How about a film?

Nick: Yes, that'd be alright.

Jenny: D'you know what's on?

Nick: No, I don't really know.

Jenny: I think I heard *Castaway's* on – it's really good, that film, you know about that woman who was sort of on a desert island.

Nick: Er well to tell the truth I've read the book and I wasn't that impressed.

Jenny: Weren't you?

Nick: Well, it sounds a bit stupid.

Jenny: Does it?

Nick: Mmm.

Jenny: Oh I'd've quite liked it. Well, never mind, let's see if there's anything else on. I'll go and get the paper. Hang on a minute.

Nick: I'll tell you what. I think *Room with a View*'s on.

Jenny: Oh yeah. I'd really like to see that. Now let's have a look. What time's the performance? Oh God, you'll never believe it.

Nick: What?

Jenny: Finished yesterday.

Nick: Oh no, what a shame!

Jenny: I'd really like to have seen that.

Nick: Er anything else on?

Jenny: Hang on, er yeah, *Colour of Money* with Paul Newman. I've sort of heard of it. What's that about?
Nick: Oh yes, he won an Oscar for it didn't he?
Jenny: Did he? Is it good?
Nick: I'm not very keen on that.
Jenny: Hang on, let's see what else is on. Arts Cinema. Oh, *Mona Lisa* at the Arts Cinema.
Nick: Oh, that'd be great, I'd like to see that.
Jenny: Well actually I've seen it. But, I wouldn't mind seeing it again, it was really good. You'll enjoy it.
Nick: Are you sure? (Yeah) What time's it on?
Jenny: Hang on, there's one – first performance 6.30, second one 8.45.
Nick: The 8.45'd be good 'cos you can book those.
Jenny: Yeah.
Nick: I'll tell you what. You give me the number and I'll ring up and book them.
Jenny: Oh, you'll book it, great. Now let's have a look. Yeah here we are, er 352001. Cambridge.
Nick: OK, alright. Well I'll ring up and book those two seats. What about some food first?
Jenny: Oh that'd be nice yeah, I'm feeling a bit hungry and I'm too tired to cook.
Nick: What about um, I know, that Chinese restaurant next to the cinema?
Jenny: Oh yeah that'd be really nice. I feel like some Chinese food tonight. That'd be lovely.
Nick: OK, well tell you what, I'll meet you um, what, seven o'clock?
Jenny: Yeah seven'd be fine, yeah.
Nick: Outside the restaurant?
Jenny: Yeah.
Nick: I'll see you there.
Jenny: OK. Bye Nick.
Nick: Bye.
Jenny: See you.

UNIT 12 A Day in the Life of . . .

Extract one: The cleaner
I start work at – I come into work at eight o'clock and the first thing I do is collect my keys, then I go down to the common room, I sweep and I wash the floor and I also check the toilets and when there's no students in the classrooms I empty the bins and do the rooms and I also help over the canteen when the girl is off, to do teas and coffees, and I usually sweep the stairs and then wash them again and I leave off at 2 o'clock.

What I particularly hate is having to be at work at a certain time and leave off at a certain time and have to work to a pattern all the while, and also I do hate cigarette ends and dirty tissues about the floor. I think there's nothing more degrading that somebody got to pick a dirty tissue up that someone's used and also to pick cigarette ends up that've been in other people's mouths. If I was to get paid for every dog end I pick up I would be a rich lady.

What I like about my job is I am free and easy. I work on my own and so if I want to do something this day I do it and if I want to do something the next day I do it. I find the students very very friendly. They will come and talk to you in their breaks or any spare time, and they will tell you all about their country, and it's very very interesting.

Extract two: A sales representative
The hours really aren't very regular although I work every day of the week Monday to Friday, but I don't start at nine till five, that sort of hours because I don't work in an office, I work from home. Having said that, some of the hours can be from seven in the morning till ten at night depending on if I get a lot of phonecalls during the week. So, having had the phonecalls I've got to go out and see them all over the place and for that, obviously, I've got to have a car, which the company supplies, er – all expenses.

Some of the people that I go to see are quite awkward; um, there are a lot of men, it's a very male-orientated business and a lot of men still feel that a woman's place is in the home and she should be tied to the kitchen sink and looking after the children.

Any candidate who comes for my type of job has to be outgoing, er fairly joyful, cheerful, they've got to be constantly smiling, eyes bright, questions answered and it's not the easiest of situations if you've had a heavy session the night before.

Extract three: A policeman
I don't really have a typical day, er all days are different but on a day for me at work it would be typical for me to go in to my office er eight o'clock and liaise with other people who I work with in my office. On commencing the patrol of my area the other thing I've got to keep my eye out open for is anything unusual in the area, any abandoned motor vehicles that may have been stolen from somewhere else or indeed anything else that should need my attention. It also involves being seen in shopping areas, areas of schools, busy crossroads, and speaking as I say, generally speaking to people, going into shops and finding out if they've got any problems or complaints.

Another part of my job is, it doesn't just revolve round crime, it does also involve reg– you know traffic regulations though there are several ways you can go about that job without always having to take the person before the courts. Warnings are often given, you don't want to, as an area community PC it's not wise to upset unnecessarily the people who you want to help you in order to do your job. This you've got to be conscious of all the time, and it takes quite a lot of skill.

UNIT 13 A Robbery

Er, let me think, it was about midday – er I'd left work early in the morning 'cos I needed to cash a cheque. Walked along to the bank er found that there weren't too many people in there, which was pretty unusual for those, for those central city banks – about ten or eleven customers. Went in, waited until it was my turn and just went up to the desk and started to talk to the bank clerk in there and he had this really strange expression on his face – he just sort of looked at me blankly – at least I thought he was looking at me and then I realised that he was staring over my shoulder and so I began to turn round, to see what he was looking at. At the same moment the guard, I mean the bank guard who, that chap outside who has a machine gun, came flying through the door and lay face down on the floor and following him through the door were three masked men, which was absolutely terrifying. I mean they had stocking, stocking masks on er which make people look really unpleasant. They were carrying guns, at least I think they all, certainly

Tapescript

the one in front was carrying a gun, a pistol. Whether or not they said anything at that point I can't remember to this day, I've just no idea or whether people just automatically put their hands up. Certainly I put my hands up er then I just didn't know what to do. For a few moments there was just total silence, suddenly broken by the telephone ringing and I remember thinking and wondering who was on the other end of the telephone. Nobody went to answer the telephone, so this thing just kept on ringing and ringing, and apart from that this, this deathly hush. Then two of the er, the masked men went to the counter in fact jumped over the counter and they had sacks with them and got the cashiers and the bank clerks to start filling the bags with cash. Anyway while the two were getting the money, the one at the door who was covering us with the gun obviously getting a bit panicky – he started swearing at them, telling them to hurry up, to get a move on. They jumped back over the counter, one of them slipped as he landed on the floor and fell over and the other two swore at him again, so it was all pretty dramatic really and then they left they left through the door. They said to us, 'Don't move, stay like that with your hands up for ten minutes'. And then they just disappeared. Again back to total silence. People put their hands down, I put my hands down but I just stayed exactly where I was. Then one of the people who worked in the bank pressed a button behind the counter and lowered the portcullis thing that you have at the front of the bank, I don't know exactly what you call it so that we were locked in and then we just stayed like that and the police arrived, I suppose after about three or four minutes, picked up the bank guard who poor chap he was still lying there prostrate on the floor and then there was a good deal of confusion and as though in a dream I just wandered out of the bank, nobody tried to stop me, the police didn't seem interested in me, they didn't want to question me, I wasn't asked to be a witness or anything so I just wandered out of the bank. Life was going on outside as normal in the busy street and I wandered back to the school. On the way back I bumped into the accountant – the school's accountant – and just sort of casually mentioned to him that I'd just been in a bank robbery; of course he was absolutely flabbergasted and said you know, 'Do you want to come for a drink?' and I said OK and in fact it was only at that point that I really began to feel nervous and almost sort of I felt myself trembling a little bit. I was a bit – I was all right later on after I'd had a couple of brandies erm, but it only really came home to me what had happened at that point. What still amazes me is that the robbers went out onto the street – which is one of the busiest streets in Naples – remember it was midday and they just disappeared into thin air. I still find that absolutely extraordinary.

UNIT 14 An Interview with Sir John

Bruce: Sir John, who lives in the house now?
Sir John: I live in the house now. I am the eighth owner since 1760 – with my staff, which consists of Mr and Mrs Naunton, my butler and my housekeeper.
Bruce: What are the duties of a butler?
Sir John: To look after my clothes, and receive people when they come to the house, tell them whether I'm here or not, er to generally befriend me, being a bachelor.

Bruce: Has the Queen been here, to Spain's Hall?
Sir John: No, the Queen has never been here, but luckily for me I've had Prince Charles here, when he was a student at Trinity College, Cambridge, and I was asked to have him to shoot and he came, and we were astonished to find what a most charming young man he was, physically much stronger than we thought – a delightful man to have as a guest, an extremely good shot, and we were all very impressed.
Bruce: When members of the royal family come here, how do you decide what they're going to eat?
Sir John: We have to find out from where they live, from the staff there, what they usually like to eat, and so we try to put on the same sort of thing, but it quite often didn't work because when Princess Margaret came to luncheon we offered her her sweet and she said she didn't want it, which rather stumped us and we had nothing much to offer in place of it. Actually she said no, but can I have please some water.
Bruce: Just some water?
Sir John: Yes, believe it or not.
Bruce: Are there any other rules you have to follow when royalty visits you?
Sir John: Yes, you're not supposed to ask them questions. You must wait until they talk to you and you can reply to their question.
Bruce: Even somebody in your position?
Sir John: Even somebody in my position, yes.
Bruce: So have you had any embarrassing moments when royalty's been here?
Sir John: Well I have actually, Bruce. When Prince Charles lunched here he suddenly said to me, 'Can I have my dog's dinner?' Well, I hadn't thought of this lovely labrador, called Flame, who lay at his feet in front of the fire while he was having lunch with me. We'd fixed up Prince Charles's lunch OK but nothing for the dog! Of course, if I'd thought about it I'd have had dog biscuits. But honour was satisfied because there was a large shooting cake in front of me on our table, lunch table and I cut a large piece off, gave it to Prince Charles, he gave it to the dog, and honour was satisfied.
Bruce: The dog liked your cake?
Sir John: Yes, wolfed it.

UNIT 15 Don't Give Up

1 in this proud land we grew up strong
we were wanted all along
I was taught to fight, taught to win
I never thought I could fail

2 no fight left or so it seems
I am a man whose dreams have all deserted
I've changed my face, I've changed my name
but no one wants you when you lose

3 don't give up
'cos you have friends
don't give up
you're not beaten yet
don't give up
I know you can make it good

4 though I saw it all around
  never thought that I could be affected
  thought that we'd be last to go
  it is so strange the way things turn

5 drove the night toward my home
  the place that I was born, on the lakeside
  as daylight broke, I saw the earth
  the trees had burned down to the ground

6 don't give up
  you still have us
  don't give up
  we don't need much of anything
  don't give up
  'cause somewhere there's a place
  where we belong

7 rest your head
  you worry too much
  it's going to be alright
  when times get rough
  you can fall back on us
  don't give up
  please don't give up

8 got to walk out of here
  I can't take any more
  going to stand on that bridge
  keep my eyes down below
  whatever may come
  and whatever may go
  that river's flowing
  that river's flowing

9 moved on to another town
  tried hard to settle down
  for every job, so many men
  so many men no one needs

10 don't give up
   cause you have friends
   don't give up
   you're not the only one
   don't give up
   no reason to be ashamed
   don't give up
   you still have us
   don't give up now
   we're proud of who you are
   don't give up
   you know it's never been easy
   don't give up
   'cause I believe there's a place
   there's a place where we belong

UNIT 16 The Supernatural

Karen: Hi Paul, what are you reading?
Paul: Oh, some daft article about a haunted house.
Karen: What do you mean, daft?
Paul: Well, it's, I dunno. They've seen some ghost there or something, I dunno.
Karen: Well, where is it?
Paul: Er, it's just down the road, in Audley End.

Karen: Well, it's old enough. What's wrong with that? There probably *are* some ghosts.
Paul: Well, I don't believe in ghosts, frankly. Do you?
Karen: Well yeah. I don't think we've got any proof that they *don't* exist. I mean, the number of people who've seen them, had experiences with them, I think it's a bit narrow-minded of you to say that there's no such thing.
Paul: Oh well, I mean I've had no evidence. I've never seen a ghost myself, and until I do I shan't believe in it.
Karen: Well, Bruce, what about you?
Bruce: I keep an open mind on it, really. Erm if people firmly believe there's such things as ghosts that's er up to them but I would never sort of scoff the idea, er I would never turn round and say oh no, it's a load of rubbish. Until you can get absolute proof one way or another, I, you know.
Paul: But you you haven't seen one yourself?
Bruce: I've never seen a ghost but er it doesn't mean to say 'cos I haven't seen one that there isn't such things. There's lots of things I haven't seen but they are about.
Karen: There's a friend of mine who's who's sort of spent all her life living with ghosts, I mean, I believe what she says and she's got stories which don't just involve her but I mean other people who've been involved with her ghosts as well.
Paul: I think people invent them. I think people want to believe in ghosts because their lives are so tedious, so boring, etc. that they invent stories. I think, I think it's a thing from the past when, you know, in the old days people believed them because they didn't have any scientific explanation for them.
Karen: Yeah, but how . . . ?
Bruce: It's like I said before, it's always difficult unless you can, I'm sure there are times when you can er give a reason for what people think is supernatural, it may not be at all, which – I agree with you on that – but I am convinced as well that there are times when the scientists can't give an adequate explanation why why this happens and and that's the time when, you know, when I think well, if, you've got to believe them in that respect, so . . .
Paul: Yes, well, I think scientists will, I mean, you take thunder and lightning. In the old days they thought that was the anger of the gods. Right? Or take something like a magnet lifting up metal, I mean it's amazing, it seemed like supernatural but now there's a scientific explanation for it.
Bruce: But there are there are stories where you get people who, like yourself, who disbelieve them and maybe even the scientists say no, that's a load of rubbish and then something happens on some occasion somewhere with them where they completely change round the opposite and they turn out to be believers.
Karen: And there's also the idea that people who so strongly disbelieve in ghosts, I mean it does seem a little bit narrow-minded but it also seems like basically they're frightened to admit there's something beyond their control. You know, I mean it could just be that you're just too frightened to admit that there's something there and you're not receptive enough, you know.
Paul: Well, that's your opinion. I shall continue to refuse to believe it until I have my own personal experience, thank you.

Tapescript

UNIT 17 Disaster

It is eight o'clock on Monday the 24th November. At least 400 people are feared to have died in a major earthquake which shook large areas of southern Italy last night. Most of the devastation has been in towns and villages outside the main cities but there has been panic in Naples too as hundreds of buildings have been destroyed. The massive rescue operation which is underway is being hampered by appalling weather conditions and a breakdown in communications.

The other headlines:

Talks are still going on in Washington in a bid to try and avert a crisis in the Gulf.

A firebomb went off in a busy shopping area in east Belfast last night killing one policeman and injuring several bystanders.

Angry teachers have voted to continue their lightning one-day strike action as pay negotiations once more break down.

And Princess Diana flies off to the sun, leaving her husband to look after the children.

As rescue work continues in wide areas of southern Italy it is becoming increasingly more likely that the present toll of 400 dead will rise much higher. The tremors were felt all over Italy, from the French border to Sicily, but the worst damage appears to be in small towns and villages, many of them very isolated, outside Naples. Naples itself has also been badly affected. In a little village about sixty miles east of the city scores of people are thought to have died as the earthquake hit a village hospital and a local church as well as many private homes. It appears that there was an evening service going on in the church at the time.

In Naples it was the old part of the city which was worst affected – many buildings of eight or nine storeys broke apart and collapsed as the earthquake hit at around eight pm last night. Panic broke out in the main prison – tear gas was used and prison officers fired machine guns into the air to try and prevent a riot. A large proportion of inhabitants spent the night in the open in the streets or squares and as smaller tremors continue more chaos has ensued as townspeople rush for the countryside, blocking roads and causing traffic jams. Telephone lines have been broken and electricity and water supplies are failing – the fog and cold conditions are making rescue operations very difficult in some of the remoter parts of the south particularly where road conditions are not very good.

Our own correspondent has been to the disaster area and sends us this report . . .

UNIT 18 Remembering My Schooldays

I was born of a working-class father and er the aspirations of many self-made men is to send their children to private boarding schools, to give them the best education money can buy, and one of the best schools in the country is Harrow.

Er Harrow is one of those institutions when I was there which at that time er were really geared to train an elite ruling class, so that everything was geared to that, and so team spirit and team games were the thing and games were really more important than the acquisition of knowledge. If you were good at er games you were considered to be er one of the heroes of the school and if you were good at work then the chances are you would be derided and laughed at as a swot or somebody who worked hard and studied hard, and that was not the attribute of a gentleman. So there were some games, like tennis, golf, were frowned on and er you were not encouraged to pursue those games but you were more encouraged to play cricket and football and Harrow football and so forth because it was required a team effort, you were one of a team you were not an individual, and it seemed to me that the public school system actually ground out the individual. You fitted into a mould, you learnt to accept certain standards. You never er showed pain, for example, you didn't er whinge about pain or discomfort and schools in my day were not comfortable places. They are now.

I think tying in with the importance of games is the fact that also that you had to be a 'man', and if people abroad think that the English gentleman is someone who is clean of limb I can assure you he's not. I think most of us washed about once a week; in winter, we used to, it was a mark of a gentleman as well that, and being tough and hard, that you didn't wear an overcoat so this meant that in winter we would pull our clothes off and the whole lot came off, shirt, several pullovers and er vests and they all came off in one go. We then put our pyjamas on and if the next morning it was particularly cold we'd just put the whole damn lot on over the pyjamas so you'd see small boys with bits of about an inch or two of pyjama trouser showing out at the bottom of their grey trousers, er, but you went, in the end, if it sort of dropped to minus ten you went around like little Michelin men with layers and layers of things on but no overcoat – that was the sign of weakness.

UNIT 19 Radio Phone-In

Announcer: Good morning. This is Nick Swift on Radio Sussex with our usual Wednesday morning phone-in. This morning the topic is you and the law, and with us in the studio is our resident solicitor, Mr Charles Andrews.

Charles: Good morning.

Announcer: Mr Andrews has been looking at some of the letters sent in by our listeners and is now ready to give us the benefit of his professional advice. And the first caller, waiting expectantly on the line is Mr Stephen Lawson from West Denham. Stephen, can you hear me?

Stephen: Yes, yes I can. Good morning, Mr Andrews.

Charles: Good morning Mr Lawson. Yes, your problem is a very common one, I'm afraid and in order to decide whether you're a protected tenant or not, legally, I mean, I'd like to ask you a few questions.

Stephen: Yeah, yeah, of course.

Charles: Now firstly, what kind of agreement do you have, if you don't mind my asking?

Stephen: Well, we haven't signed anything, if that's what you mean – er, we've got a rent book and we pay rent every month.

Charles: Ah, you do have a rent book, and you pay every month. Does the landlord live on the premises?

Stephen: No, no, in fact we hardly ever see him, he lives in another part of the country.

Charles: So he doesn't provide any services for you – by that I mean, breakfast, linen, that kind of thing?

Stephen: (laughing) No, nothing like that – unfortunately.

Charles: Ah, well, actually it is better for you that he doesn't. Now he's written to you formally asking you to leave, I take it?

Stephen: No, no, he just keeps phoning up and keeping on at us – it's really getting us down.

Charles: Yes, quite so. Well a couple of things there. Firstly, he must inform you in writing, or else it's not legal. And after that, since you pay monthly he's got to give you a month before you leave anyway. Now secondly, he's not allowed to keep pestering you like this until he has got a court order for possession – you could sue him for harassment.

Stephen: Oh, I see, that's interesting to know.

Charles: Now do you happen to know his reasons for wanting to regain possession of the house?

Stephen: No, we assumed he wanted to sell or something, but . . .

Charles: Yes, because if he needs it for himself or a member of his family then I'm afraid you've got problems. Otherwise it seems to me that you've probably got a pretty good chance of staying put, at least for a year or so.

Stephen: That would be wonderful, because we leave college then, anyway.

Charles: But er, I have to say that this whole issue is so complex that you'd be better off going and speaking to a solicitor in more detail. We haven't got time in this phone call to cover everything, I'm afraid.

Stephen: OK, well thanks very much.

Charles: And remember if you're a student you are protected by Legal Aid, which means you don't have to pay the fees yourself.

Stephen: Great! Thanks again.

Announcer: I'm sure Stephen is much more optimistic already. Next on the line is Mrs Mary Peters from Townley and she has a problem with a jacket she wants to return to the shop.

Mary: Hello.

Charles: Hello Mrs Peters. Yes, I think your case may be a little more simple. The main question is, was there anything wrong with the jacket at all, was it faulty in any way?

Mary: No, it was just too small – it was my mistake.

Charles: Ah yes, because in that case I'm afraid they're right, they are not legally obliged to give you your money back or even exchange on sales items. However, if the goods are faulty in any way then they *must*, sale or no sale.

Mary: So there's nothing I can do?

Charles: I'm afraid not Mrs Peters. Actually, I think you were unfortunate. Most big department stores would at least have given you a credit note as long as you had a receipt and had returned the item fairly soon after the purchase. It's not worth having bad customer relations, you see.

Mary: No, this was quite a small shop. Oh well, not to worry. Thanks anyway for your time – I'll know next time, won't I?

Charles: Yes, you certainly will.

UNIT 20   Places I Know

Extract one: **Pat**

Every year for the last few years we've visited our friends in a small tiny tiny little village in the middle of France and they bought a cowshed and it was literally a cowshed with, not fit to live in and they have gradually made it better and renovated it and it's in a beautiful position – it's on the top of a hill and for miles around you can see this beautiful countryside, and I think only one other house so you do need a car er and you take the car into the tiny little village where there are about four or five shops and a very nice restaurant where you can go and have a five course meal for very little money and also near is a very big lake – because this place is in the Dordogne and there are lots of lakes there and we go there most afternoons and windsurf and sail.

Also there's a very nice market French market there once a week where you get lovely pâtés, lovely fresh fish, really good fresh fish and lovely bowls and baskets which the local people have made. I like this part of France very much but I think it's a shame that there are too many English people there.

Extract two: **David**

What kind of city is it? It's a very modern city. I expected that Tokyo would be quite old but there are very few parts of it which are old in fact at all because it was firebombed during the second World War by the Americans, there are one or two temples that survived that but basically it's a city that's been built since 1945. Um, a lot of it is low rise; one-, two-, three-storey houses because of the earthquake danger, 'cos they get lots of earthquakes.

Once you've mastered a little bit of Japanese it's relatively easy to get around Tokyo because they've got an excellent subway system and it's quick and easy to get around. The problem is of course that Tokyo is a city of thirteen, fourteen, fifteen million people and they all want to get around at exactly the same time, er, so especially if you're travelling in the rush hours, eight o'clock in the morning, five o'clock at night it is a question in many of the big stations of being pushed on to the train – they pay students a bit of extra pocket money to do this. Right in the centre of Tokyo is the Imperial Palace, and that's set in delightful gardens, but it's completely closed to the public so nobody ever sees it. In the rest of Tokyo there are ten, twelve public gardens but they tend to get very filled up with people, especially during national holidays and what have you. Other than that it's just street after street and block after block of very similar houses, as I say one- or two-storeyed houses – which just go on and on for mile after mile because Tokyo extends over – I don't know – hundreds of square miles – a massive city.

Extract three: **Cindy**

I come from a place – I come from the northern United States, Rochester, Minnesota – it's a town of about 50,000 people and it's a very very clean town, it's an ordinary town, fairly wealthy, but it's a bit strange because there are a lot of transients – a lot of people who don't live there. It's the home of the Mayo clinic, and so there are thousands and thousands of people who come every year. The other thing is there're also a lot of foreign residents – a lot of doctors and nurses are from other countries and so it makes what could be a really dull mid-west town something special. The library's very good – cultural events are much more interesting than the rest of Minnesota and actually it's not a bad place to grow up. On the other hand I was dying to leave there and all I could think of was getting away from the mid-west and the cold winters – you have about six months when it's almost too cold to go outside. A lot of the buildings are designed so that you can walk from one to the other underground. There's a big pedestrian subway system so you can avoid all this snow.

Teachers' notes

UNIT 1   A New Job

This unit could be linked thematically to Unit 3 (Snakes and Other Animals), to Unit 12 (A Day in the Life of . . .) and to Unit 15 (Don't Give Up).

PART B   Listening activities

Question 5) is intended as an information gap activity; student A fills in Sue's notes and student B fills in John Adams's memo and then they work in pairs to fill in the information they haven't got. (NB Make sure the students write *notes*.)

If the students do question 6) first as a prediction exercise (before listening), make sure they realise that there are several possibilities for a) and c) and the version on the tape is not the only correct one.

Exercises a) and c) focus on functional language, whereas b) focuses on present perfect tenses (indefinite time and duration) and might usefully serve for revision purposes.

Optional activities

* focus on stress patterns, weak forms and intonation in the intensive listening part. Students could mark features of connected speech, such as stress patterns, and then practise reading it in pairs.
* roleplay the interview between Sue and John Adams.

PART C   Writing task

This could be preceded by information on how to write formal letters:
* layout
* opening and closing conventions, salutations, etc.
* language used to talk about experience, qualifications, hobbies, etc.
* other suggestions about content

Optional activities

* exchange letters of application around the class and decide which person you would employ, and why.
* give the students different job adverts, and get them to apply for the one they are interested in.

UNIT 2   Julia's Strange Experience (1)

This unit comes before Unit 10 (which is the second part of the story) and would go well with Unit 16 (The Supernatural).

PART A   Before you listen

Elicit/pre-teach the vocabulary connected with the sound sequence on the tape (see key).

Encourage discussion of the story in groups to arouse motivation and develop fluency skills. If there is time, ask the groups to give their stories to the class. This is a possible opportunity to do remedial work on past tense sequences, revise/teach linking words and practise expressions such as *it could be/it may be.*

PART B   Optional activities

* work on past simple versus past progressive verbs (which of the verbs in COLUMN B could take the progressive form. Why/Why not?)
* pronunciation of past simple verbs (t/d)

PART C   Writing task

This could be done as a 'chain' writing story around the class, with each student writing one line.

UNIT 3   Snakes and Other Animals

This unit could be used in conjunction with other ones talking about jobs, e.g. Units 1 and 12.

PART A   Before you listen

The aim of texts A and B is to generate discussion on attitudes to pets, and encourage students to give opinions/agree and disagree with each other. Try also to elicit names of pets (the ones that come up in the text are snakes, parrots, rats, ferrets, budgerigars) and what RSPCA means.

PART B   Listening activities

Question 4) could be a useful way of revising reported speech (i.e. He said . . .).

PART C   Writing task

Another optional writing text could be the pros and cons of keeping a particular pet, written as a discursive essay, or writing description of a pet.

UNIT 4   Street Life

PART A   Before you listen

Encourage discussion of the photograph and try to elicit (otherwise pre-teach) words such as cottage, terraced house, next-door neighbour, gossip, thin walls, etc.).

PART C   Writing task

Alternatively, the students could write a short summary of life in Mill Lane, for a magazine or newspaper in their own country.

UNIT 5   My Kind of Sport

This unit could be linked to other units on spare time/leisure (Units 6 and 11).

UNIT 6   Holiday Plans

This could be tied in with Unit 11 (A Night Out) and Unit 20 (Places I Know).

PART A   Before you listen

The questionnaire at the beginning should highlight some useful vocabulary connected with holidays (make sure they know *self-catering*) and teach/revise the language of preference (*Would you rather/Do you prefer + ing*).

Optional activity

* write a 'solution' for the questionnaire.

PART B   Optional activity

* interview people in their class about their holiday plans and write up the interview using the appropriate form of the future.

PART C   Writing task

Draw attention to the convention of postcard writing, especially the frequent omission of personal pronouns.

UNIT 7 Frightening Experiences

This unit would tie in thematically with Unit 13 (A Robbery) and Unit 17 (Disaster).

PART A Before you listen
This text aims to teach the vocabulary of disasters which comes up in the text, but it also lends itself to discussing the language of headlines and the style of different newspapers (compare extract 1 with 2 and 3).
Question 3) gives extra work on present perfect and passive forms and this could be extended, if you wish, by asking students to read through the text and underline when the simple past/present perfect/past perfect is used, and to come to some conclusion about the use of these tenses (see also Unit 17).

Optional activity
● extra work on comparing different newspaper styles in the British press.

PART C Writing task
Encourage students to adopt a particular style (formal or informal) in their report.

Optional activity
● ask the students to write a story based on headlines you give them.

UNIT 8 Are You a Good Language Learner

PART A Before you listen
Encourage discussion as much as possible and explain terminology the students don't know. The discussion should involve use of modals such as *don't need to/have to/ should*, etc. and should generate opinion giving, agreeing and disagreeing.

UNIT 9 Children Talking

PART A Before you listen
The discussion generated by the picture should include use of:
● language of past habits (*used to/would . . .*)
● comparative forms

PART B Listening activities
Encourage the students to write *notes* for question 5) and get them to report back. (There could be an optional focus on what they like doing, to revise verbs followed by gerund.)
Question 6) focuses on modals such as *have to/make . . . do* and on *to be allowed to*.

UNIT 10 Julia's Strange Experience (2)

This unit comes after Unit 2 and fits well with Unit 16.

PART A Before you listen
Play the first part of the tape up to 'looking at her kindly' and encourage discussion of what happens next, in groups or as a class.
You may like to discuss the stories they wrote at the end of Unit 2 since this, also, is a prediction of this story.

PART B Listening activities
Questions 3) and 4) help to make students aware of how indirect speech is formed and what happens when there are reporting verbs such as *apologise* and *offer*. Additional work could be done on this.

UNIT 11 A Night Out

This unit fits well with Unit 6 (Holiday Plans).

PART B Listening activities
An optional activity for question 5) would be to get students to mark contracted forms or stress patterns, etc. as they are listening, and practise reading the dialogues using the tape as a model.

Optional activity
● act out or write a similar dialogue.

UNIT 12 A Day in the Life of . . .

This unit could be integrated with Units 1 and 3 and Unit 15.

PART A Before you listen
The discussion could include comparisons, and use of modal verbs to describe what you have to do/need to do, etc.

PART B Listening activities
In question 6), draw the students' attention to the unusual use of *will* for describing regular habits.

UNIT 13 A Robbery

This unit would go well with Units 7 and 17.

PART A Before you listen
There is certain vocabulary which comes up in the listening text and which should be highlighted in the reading text, such as *burglary*, *armed*, *stocking mask*, etc.

Optional activity
● work on descriptions of people.

PART B While listening
Optional work could be done on sequencing of past tenses (e.g. *What was he doing when they came in? He told the accountant what had happened*).

PART C Writing task
Input may be needed on how to write a report so that it is brief and clear.

UNIT 14 An Interview with Sir John

PART A Before you listen
While discussing the picture, try to elicit vocabulary such as *aristocracy*, *royalty*, *butler*, etc.

PART B While listening
In question 5, extra work could be done on modals, and past conditional forms.

PART C Writing task

It may be necessary to give the students some ideas first as to the choice of menu, and topics of conversation.

UNIT 15 This Proud Land

This unit could be linked to Units 1, 3 and 12.

PART A Before you listen

The aim in questions 1) and 3) is to encourage interpretation of the text and for students to share their opinions, preferably in pairs or groups. Fluency is therefore much more important than accuracy, and it is important to stress to them that there is no *one* correct answer. It may be necessary to discuss with them the different meanings of *proud* and *fight* and the difference between *win* and *beat*. Question 2) should also encourage discussion on how you predict the order based on cohesion.

PART B Listening activities

In question 4), play only the first part of the song (until the end of verse 7 in the transcript. Encourage discussion on the relationship between the two people, but it is very likely that they will not be able to do question 5) until they have completed question 6).
Question 6) is best done in the language laboratory if you have one, as it requires very intensive listening.

Optional activities

- a variation for question 6) is to change some of the words so that they are similar in pronunciation, and get the students to spot them, and change them, e.g. *here* becomes *beer* or *near*, *that* becomes *bat* or *fat*, etc.)

Optional activity

- give students the tapescript of the song with certain features of connected speech underlined to make them aware of such typical features as weak forms, contractions, assimilation, etc. For example you could underline:
  - *don't give up* = dəʊn'gɪvʌp
  - *trees had* = zəd
  - *going to* = gənə

  and the weak forms of *the* and *a*.
  You could also try to get them to mark the stress patterns in the first few verses.
  Question 7) could be extended to include brainstorming on other phrasal/prepositional verbs the students know.

UNIT 16 The Supernatural

This unit links with Units 2 and 10.

PART A Before you listen

The questionnaire introduces some new vocabulary which should lead to a discussion on beliefs. Try to elicit vocabulary such as *narrow-minded, daft, load of rubbish, proof*, etc. to lighten the load in the listening text.

UNIT 17 Disaster

This unit goes well with Units 7 and 13.

PART A Before you listen

Use the picture to elicit vocabulary such as *collapse, devastation, tremor*, etc.

PART B While listening

Question 4) focuses on the form, and especially the use of present and past passive forms. You could also focus on present perfect/past tense forms.

PART C Writing task

You could also get the students to write up each other's dialogues as an article for the newspaper, to practise reported speech.

UNIT 18 Remembering My Schooldays

PART A Before you listen

Use the picture to introduce the concept of public schools, boarding schools, etc. after discussing question 1).

PART B Listening activities

Attention could be drawn to Tim's way of talking about past habits using *would*, in the last part of the tape.

UNIT 19 Radio Phone-In

PART A Before you listen

Discussion of answers for the letters could usefully be done in groups. They may need help with some of the vocabulary.

PART C Writing task

It would be useful to begin with input on the language of advice (e.g. *If I were you; should; had better*, etc.).

UNIT 20 Places I Know

This unit would go well with Units 6 and 11.

PART A Before you listen

You could focus on conditional forms in question 2) for hypothetical/unreal situations.

PART C Writing task

The teacher could provide input/models on descriptions of places.

Answer key

UNIT 1

2) a) A store (store, merchandise, customer, shop)
   b) Taking care of staff; maintaining catering standards; running the staff dining room; preparing simple hot and cold meals
   c) Write to, or phone, the Personnel Officer

3) Examples: salary, hours, benefits, number of staff, holidays

5) A Salary: £75(+) per week
   Hours: from 10 am to 2 pm
   Duties: preparing and serving food at lunchtime
   Number of staff: 15 to 20
   Interview? When?: Wednesday 2.30

   B Surname: Ms Boardman
   Name: S (Sue)
   Catering experience: 5 years
   Present employer: Bloggs
   Employer's job: consultant engineers
   Interview time/date: Wednesday 2.30

6) and 7)
   a) **Operator:** Hello, Woolworth's.
      Sue: Ah hello. I wonder *if I could speak to* the Personnel Manager, please?
      Operator: Yes, certainly. If *you'll hold on* a minute I'll put you through.
      Sue: Thank you.
   b) **John Adams:** *Have you (in fact) had any* experience in catering?
      Sue: Yes, . . . I'm at present working for, and *have been working for* the same firm for about five years, for a small firm of consultant engineers, and *I've been doing* work rather similar to the kind described in the advertisement.
   c) **John Adams:** Perhaps *you could come down* for an interview some time?
      Sue: Yes, when *would be suitable* for you?
      John Adams: *What about* next Wednesday?
      Sue: Yes, I think *that would be* fine, actually.

UNIT 2

1) Sound sequence: wind howling; pouring rain; crash of thunder/storm; car stopping/braking; music on stereo; car door opening; someone getting out of car; cat miaowing; getting back into car; trying to start car; rustling of clothes; heavy breathing/snoring; footsteps; car door opening; scream

3) a) False   f) True
   b) True   g) False
   c) False   h) False
   d) False   i) True
   e) False   j) False

4) i) e   v) d
   ii) g   vi) b
   iii) f   vii) a
   iv) c

5) a) The rain *beat against the windscreen.*
   b) The trees *swayed in the wind.*
   c) The lightning *lit up the sea.*

   d) Julia *shivered.*
   e) Julia *screamed.*
   f) Julia *switched off the engine.*
   g) Julia *turned up the music.*
   h) Julia *picked up the torch.*
   i) The cat *stretched.*
   j) Someone *was opening the passenger door.*

UNIT 3

3) The topics which were discussed were:
   - how people treat pets
   - the good things about being a vet
   - snakes
   - the dangers of his job
   - how pets can be good for you
   - the sort of animals he looks after

4) Mr Mercer is a very experienced veterinary surgeon. He is qualified to deal with many different kinds of animals – either in his surgery or in various places like zoos and [1]the jungle. He is particularly fond of snakes and [2]keeps one as a pet. He admires them because they are strong and muscular and [3]he finds them useful for frightening other people with. They once had to deal with a snake that was [4]fifteen feet long; [5]Mr Mercer was worried in case it bit him.
   He feels that [6]far too many people treat their pets too well. Some of them even kiss them. However, he believes that animals are particularly useful as companions for old people; they perform the function of friends and they can be with them the whole time. [7]He particularly recommends budgerigars as pets for old people. When animals come to his surgery they are often frightened and can become aggressive. [8]He is always being hurt – sometimes badly – by dogs and cats.
   Mr Mercer enjoys his job and the variety it gives him. He enjoys working in his surgery, [9]working in his office and going out on visits. His greatest love, however, is helping animals to give birth.

UNIT 4

1) Cottages

2) Terraced houses

5) Extract one: e   Extract four: a
   Extract two: c   Extract five: d
   Extract three: b

6) a) iii)   d) iii)
   b) iii)   e) ii)
   c) ii)   f) iii)

7) Disagrees: Well no, I don't agree wholly there . . .
   Agrees: I suppose I agree with you there, as far as . . .

8) - blind drunk: the ex-husband
   - stone deaf: Peter's next-door neighbour (husband)
   - shrieking at the top of her voice: Peter's next-door neighbour (wife)
   - on at each other: the next-door neighbours
   - a nightbird: Peter's neighbour opposite
   - well-looked-after: the old people in the lane
   - would go berserk if the dog made messes in their gardens: cat owners

UNIT 5

1) A: (to play) tennis
   B: (to play) football
   C: (to go) cycling
   D: (to play) squash
   E: (to go) skiing
   F: (to go) sailing

5) Extract one: Jo D
   Extract two: Brian B
   Extract three: Stephanie E

6) • needs a lot of energy   squash
   • is exciting   football
   • can be dangerous   skiing
   • is very popular at the moment   squash
   • is fast   skiing
   • requires skill   football/skiing
   • can you not play for a long time
     because it's tiring   squash
   • is expensive   skiing

7)

	Jo	Brian	Stephanie
a)	Since she was at school/quite young	For nearly forty years/ever since he was a little kid	Since she can remember
b)	Yes	Yes	Yes

c) Jo: I've been playing it since I was at school – since I was quite young.
   Brian: I've been playing for nearly forty years, ever since I was a little kid.
   Stephanie: I've been doing it every winter holiday since I can remember.

UNIT 6

4) Alistair: a (culture)
   Barbara: b (beaches, sun and sea)
   Mike: c (countryside)

5)

		Where	Plans?
a)	Alistair	Italy (Milan)	Cultural holiday, museums/ art galleries, driving around, tasting food/drink
b)	Barbara	Tenerife? Greece?	Relax, lie on beach
c)	Mike	England (Lake District)	Stay in small country cottage (self-catering), walking holiday

6) Alistair: I'm leaving at eight tomorrow morning
   Barbara: I may go to Tenerife/might go to Greece
   Mike: I'll go out in the car

UNIT 7

1) 1 B   3 D   5 F
   2 E   4 A   6 C

4) A bus crash

5) a) True   e) True   i) False
   b) False   f) False   j) False
   c) True   g) False
   d) False   h) True

UNIT 8

3) Point one: Motivation
   Point two: Personality
   Point three: Learning skills
   Point four: Independence

4) Independence

5) **The Good Language Learner**

1 out of the classroom
2 external
3 schoolchildren studying for examinations
4 immigrants
5 speed
6 extrovert
7 confident
8 having a good ear
9 own speech
10 orgnisation of learning
11 most important
12 teacher
13 responsibility
14 progress

UNIT 9

4) • free time   3   • food   6
   • music   2   • bedtime   4
   • pocket money   1   • rules   5
   • going abroad   7

5)

	Simon	Louisa
How much pocket money do they get?	£4 per week	£1 per week
What do they spend it on?	Computer games, pencils, pens, sweets, cars, footballs	Tapes, records
How do they spend their spare time?	Football, computer, TV, music, sport	Clean out guinea pig, play with dog, swim, play tennis, football
What time do they go to bed?	8 pm (weekdays) 10 pm (weekends)	8 pm
Are there any other rules at home?	Eating vegetables, not playing football in back garden, not leaving toys around	Not eating white bread/rice
Have they been abroad? If so, where?	Austria	Portugal, France, Italy

6) • going to bed { during the week — I have to go to bed very very early. / at the weekend — I'm allowed to go to bed quite late.
   • eating the food he doesn't like — They make me eat all the food. I don't like any vegetables and I have to eat them.
   • playing football in the back garden — I'm not allowed to play . . .
   • leaving his toys around — I'm not allowed to leave my toys . . .

UNIT 10

1) 2 D   4 A   6 G   8 B
   3 H   5 E   7 C

2) The person who opened the door was a woman of [1]*about twenty*, wearing [2]*a raincoat* and a bright [3]*blue* scarf around her [4]*head* to protect her from the rain. She looked quite friendly, so Julia asked her if she knew of [5]*a house* where she could phone from, and the woman offered to show her.

They walked off [6]*together*, not saying very much, and then they saw [7]*a large house* with [8]*the lights still on*, even though it was well after midnight. The woman [9]*rang the bell* and then [10]*explained the situation* to the old man who answered the door.

1 in her forties	6 the woman ahead
2 an overcoat	7 a small cottage
3 red	8 dark
4 neck	9 knocked
5 a phonebox	10 disappeared

3) a) 'My car won't start.'
   b) 'Do you know if there's a phonebox near here?'
   c) 'I'll take you to a house.'
   d) 'I'm sorry to wake you up.'
   e) 'Come in, come in.'
   f) 'I don't have any children.'

UNIT 11

3) Friday

4) a) ii)   b) iii)   c) ii)   d) iii)

5) a) Jenny suggests seeing a film: *How about a film?*
     Nick agrees: *Yes, that'd be alright.*
     Jenny doesn't know what films there are: *D'you know what's on?*
     She asks him to wait (while she gets the paper): *Hang on a minute.*
   b) Nick offers to book seats: *I'll ring up and book them.*
     He suggests food first: *What about some food first?*
     Jenny agrees: *Oh, that'd be nice.*
     Nick ends the conversation: *I'll see you there. Bye.*

6) a) Oh no, what a shame!
   b) I'm not very keen on that.
   c) Oh, that'd be great.

UNIT 12

3)

Examples:	Job	Key words
Extract one: Ivy	Cleaner in a college	sweep, wash the floor, empty bins, do rooms, pick up cigarette ends, dirty tissues
Extract two: Heather	Sales representative	work from home, phone calls, go out and see them all over the place
Extract three: Stephen	Policeman	commence patrol, abandoned motor vehicles, crime/traffic regulations, area community PC

4) a) Hours: 8 am–2 pm
     Duties: sweep and wash floor, check toilets, empty bins, do rooms, help in canteen, sweep and wash stairs
     Advantages of job: free and easy, friendly students
     Disadvantages of job: routine hours/work, picking up cigarette ends and dirty tissues

   b) Hours: Mon–Fri irregular hours
     Duties: receiving phone calls, visiting people
     Personality necessary for job: outgoing, cheerful, smiling
     Advantages: car with job (all expenses), flexible hours
     Disadvantages: awkward clients, needing always to be lively, sometimes long hours

   c)

1 into the office	5 shopping areas
2 eight	6 crossroads
3 unusual	7 problems
4 motor vehicles	8 warning

UNIT 13

1) a) He's suspected of committing several burglaries.
   b) A woman who was tied up in her own home.
   c) In his late twenties.
   d) A stocking mask.
   e) He could be armed.

3) ● What kind of robbery was it?   *a bank robbery*
   ● Was it a successful robbery?   *yes*
   ● How did Tony feel   a) during it?   *fairly calm*
                      b) after it?   *calm then nervous*

4) a) Midday
   b) Central city (Naples)
   c) Ten or eleven
   d) Talking to the bank clerk
   e) Three
   f) Stocking masks
   g) Guns (pistols)
   h) He can't remember
   i) Put their hands up
   j) Jumped over counter and got the bank clerks and cashiers to fill sacks
   k) Don't move. Stay with your hands up for ten minutes
   l) Three or four minutes after someone pressed the alarm
   m) Wandered out of the bank towards the school, met accountant and went for a drink

5) i) d)   iii) h)   v) e)   vii) f)   xi) i
   ii) a)   iv) c)   vi) g)   viii) b)

UNIT 14

3) b) Important guests he has had

4) a) 3: Sir John, Mr and Mrs Naunton
   b) ● look after clothes
       ● receive people
       ● befriend him
   c) Charming, delightful, a good shot, he was impressed
   d) To shoot
   e) She didn't want her sweet (dessert)
   f) You must wait until they talk to you
   g) Because of Sir John's position
   h) Sir John hadn't any lunch for Charles's dog
   i) By giving the dog some of the shooting cake

5 *Example answers:*
   a) you shouldn't . . .; it's better not to . . .; you're not
      meant to . . .
   b) If I'd realised she didn't like the sweet I'd have got
      other ones as well.

6) i) c)   ii) d)   iii) b)   iv) e)   v) a)

UNIT 15

1) a) Could include failing an exam, getting divorced, etc.,
     as well as the 'real' answer, unemployment.
   b) *Example adjectives*: desperate, rejected, alone,
     humiliated, etc.
   c) Presumably a fairly secure one ('we were wanted all
     along') and where success and competition were
     important ('taught to fight/win'). He was never taught
     to think or dream of rejection or failure.
   d) In an ironic sense: 'proud' meaning wonderful, but
     also perhaps, the land itself is too proud to admit
     failure.
   e) Unemployment
   Note: It is important to emphasise that these are not
   necessarily the 'correct' answers – these are only
   interpretations.

2) The correct order is: a) 3)   b) 1   c) 2   d) 4

3) This verse tells us that he acted spontaneously ('drove
   the night') and is perhaps nostalgic for his childhood, or
   his past. The 'burned trees' perhaps refer to his 'dreams
   which have deserted' and the feeling of instability.

4) b) Don't give up

6) 1 walk   6 whatever   11 town
   2 take   7 whatever   12 down
   3 stand   8 river   13 job
   4 bridge   9 river   14 needs
   5 eyes   10 moved

7) a) burned down   c) settle down   e) fall back
   b) grew up   d) gave up   f) move on

UNIT 16

3) a) Superstition f   e) Poltergeists   a
   b) Palmistry   h   f) Telepathy   d
   c) Astrology   c   g) Fortune telling b
   d) Ghosts   g   h) Graphology   e

4) a) Ghosts (g)

5) a) Karen   c) Bruce   e) Paul   g) Karen
   b) Karen   d) Paul   f) Bruce

6) i)   g)   iv) h)   vii) b) or d)
   ii) b) or d)   v) f)   viii) i)
   iii) a)   vi) e)   ix) c)

UNIT 17

1) a) An earthquake

2) a) An earthquake
   b) On 23rd November in southern Italy

3) 1 Tremors   6 Telephone
   2 four hundred   7 rescue
   3 died   8 weather
   4 Hundreds   9 prison
   5 villages   10 rush

4) 1 was shaken   4 have been broken
   2 are thought   5 are being delayed
   3 have been destroyed   6 was used

UNIT 18

3) c) to produce 'gentlemen'

4) You needed to:
   • be 'masculine'   • be good at sport
   • mix well with other boys • be able to lead/
   • conform   influence others

5) To be able to lead others   To be good at sport

6) Tim probably did not conform or lead others (he was
   probably more of an individual).

7) 1 swot   4 frowned on   7 hard
   2 team   5 pain   8 overcoat
   3 hero   6 tough   9 dropped

UNIT 19

1) A b) B a)   C b)

2) First caller: B
   Second caller: A

3) a) 1 obliged   3 sale   5 receipt
       2 exchange   4 credit note
   b) 1 signed   4 provides   7 tenant
       2 rent   5 month
       3 landlord   6 his family

UNIT 20

3)

	Likes	Dislikes
Extract one: Pat	House in beautiful position, nice restaurant, market, lovely food, bowls/baskets	Too many English people
Extract two: David	Excellent subway system	In rush hour, too many people
Extract three: Cindy	Clean/healthy, lots of foreign residents, good library, cultural events	The cold

4) Extract one: Extract two:
   a) Every year   a) Post 1945
   b) Tiny   b) Because of earthquakes
   c) A cowshed   c) Students push you on
   d) Windsurfing, sailing   d) They're full of people
   e) Bowls/baskets   e) Massive
   Extract three:
   a) There are lots of transients
   b) No
   c) Not bad
   d) She was dying to go
   e) By using the pedestrian subway system